The
Scots and China
1750 – 2000
ISSUES IDEAS AND IDENTITIES

D1343985

Ian Wotherspoon

Aberdeenshire

3117463

ISBN-10: 1481025503

EAN-13: 9781481025508

Library of Congress Control Number: 2012922007
CreateSpace Independent Publishing Platform
North Charleston, South Carolina

For
Zack and Ruairidh

Contents

Throughout this book, the pinyin system of romanization has been used for Chinese place names, proper names etc. However, I have normally shown older forms of romanization on the first occasion a name is given as these may be more familiar to some readers. Thus, for example, Guangzhou is first given as Guangzhou (Canton); similarly, the writer Jiang Yi is first given as Jiang Yi (Chiang Yee).

Some of the material used in Chapters 3 and 6 was published in 2004 and 2006 in *Sine*, the Journal of the Scotland-China Association.

1 Prologue - the Scots and China

If (the Chinese) are ever to be further improved,
it must be by foreigners.

JOHN STUART MILL.

I first went to China over forty years ago, flying across the Pearl
River delta into what was known as the Crown Colony of Hong
Kong – a borrowed place on borrowed time. Then, Hong Kong was
pulling itself slowly together after a series of riots spawned by Mao
Zedong's Cultural Revolution which convulsed China in the 1960s.
The arrogance and intransigence of the colony's British administration,
which had responded too slowly to what were very legitimate concerns
about squalid housing, social conditions and sleaze, contributed to these
tensions. However, a new Governor, a Scot called Murray MacLehose,
had just been appointed and was making progress in modernising
Hong Kong's byzantine public service, firmly rooting out corruption
and promoting one of the largest, and most extensive, public housing
programmes in Asia.

MacLehose was not the first Scot to have close connections with China,
or make an impact on that country's destiny. During the bitter years of
western intervention in China, Scottish institutions, ideas and people
had close associations with Chinese affairs, certainly up to 1949 when
the People's Republic was inaugurated but, arguably, beyond through
the medium of British administration in Hong Kong.

1

Scottish interest in China extended from trade and commerce to banking and finance as well as to the development of China's economic infrastructure. It also covered the promotion of western educational ideas and models, and the scientific exploration of China's environment, flora and fauna, plus seriously determined efforts to harvest souls for Christ in a largely Confucian culture. These connections provided a conduit for western political ideas and influence, not just in Hong Kong and the treaty ports - cities in China opened to foreign settlement and commerce after 1842 - but, more generally, in the wider context of growing Chinese nationalist sentiment, as exemplified in the Boxer rising of 1900, the response to the 1931 Japanese invasion of China and the civil war that followed.

As elsewhere in the formal and informal British Empire in the nineteenth and twentieth centuries, Scots in China operated from a variety of social, economic and religious platforms – some from more than one. Many of the influences Scots exercised in China during this period were ephemeral, a few more long lasting.

Scots as different as William Jardine, the opium trader, and Dugald Christie, the medical missionary in Shenyang (Mukden), brought a very Scottish dimension to their engagement with China. So did Thomas Sutherland who introduced Scottish (as opposed to English) banking practice to China. Others were involved in the government and administration of China. James Stewart Lockhart was the first Civil Commissioner of Weihaiwei (today's Weihai) on the coast of Shandong Province from 1902 to 1921. Lockhart worked with Edinburgh-born Reginald Johnston who was later appointed tutor to Puyi, the former Emperor. Half a century later, the redoubtable MacLehose, Governor of Hong Kong from 1971 to 1982, brought to his work a directness, enthusiasm and urgency that would have been well understood by his fellow Scots, past and present. Not for nothing was he known as "Jock the Sock" which wasn't just a play on his name!

By the end of the eighteenth century the Scottish economy was benefitting from the outcome of the union in 1707 of the English and Scottish Parliaments which allowed Scots access, not only to markets in England itself, but also to those of the expanding British Empire overseas. Scottish loyalty to the new British state had been reinforced by Walpole, and his successors, who provided opportunities for Scots to trade, and prosper, in locations as diverse as the Caribbean, Bengal and along the eastern seaboard of colonial America. As business skills were honed, a network of Scottish trading connections began to emerge – by the end of the nineteenth century it stretched from Beijing (Peking) to Buenos Aires and from Madras to Montreal.

Scotland was well placed to take advantage of the opportunities offered by exposure to a wider world. Scots had always been on the move in Europe as soldiers, traders, agriculturalists, scholars and industrial pioneers, so engagement overseas was not seen as something novel or unusual. Scotland's then five universities produced a surplus of talented manpower which readily sought employment elsewhere in Britain, or abroad - their expertise in medicine was quickly recognised, and valued, particularly in the army and navy. Through political patronage, or sheer hard work, they secured a disproportionate number of appointments in the great trading houses of the day whether that was the Hudson's Bay Company, in what was to become Canada, or the British East India Company (EIC) in Bengal.

Scotland was one of the first countries in Europe to embrace industrialisation and progressively developed a diversified and skilled workforce able to meet the needs of growing economies around the world. By the 1750s Glasgow had emerged as the largest entrepot port in Britain, re-exporting ninety per cent of tobacco imported from America. A century and a half later, Glasgow had become the second city of the British Empire, and the sixth largest in the world, producing marine engines, railway locomotives and rolling stock, not to mention steel and chemicals. A third of the vessels then built in Britain came from the Clyde whose products set the benchmark for quality and reliability.

So successful were the Scots commercially, and in penetrating all areas of government and education, that English hostility was never far below the surface. Scots were often seen as clannish, self-seeking, and shrewd – perhaps not without justification. The Scots may have been equally disdainful of the English but quickly became enthusiastic imperialists. In almost all cases the Bible read in a Scots tongue followed commerce and the sword, whether that was in Africa, India or China.

Scotland's growing world outreach through emigration and trade would have been of little interest to the Qianlong Emperor, who reigned from 1736 to 1796, or his conservative autocracy. Developments in the barbarian west were seen more as an irritant - China was, they believed, the "middle kingdom" at the centre of the world with little need for the ideas, goods or services the west might offer.

Responding in 1793 to British proposals to liberalise trade between the two countries, the Emperor wrote to George lll that "Our dynasty's majestic virtue has penetrated into every country under Heaven ... I set no value on objects strange or ingenious, and have no use for your country's manufactures..."[1] Little did the Emperor realise that what would give the west competitive advantage was James Watt's "ingenious" steam engine, which would power the nineteenth century, and propel China into contact with an often menacing, barbarian world.

Despite the Emperor's opposition, trade between China and the west expanded throughout the eighteenth century. From China came porcelain, silk and, most importantly, tea. These trading connections spawned a growing awareness in Scotland, as elsewhere in the west, of Chinese political and social issues as well as of Chinese customs, thinking and learning. Leaders of the European Enlightenment, like Voltaire, believed that China had much to offer the west given its emphasis on rationalism and stable rule. The doughty David Hume in Edinburgh agreed, but with reservations. "In China, there seems to be a pretty considerable stock of politeness and science, which, in the course of so many centuries, might naturally be expected to ripen into something more perfect and finished, than what has yet arisen from them."[2] The reason it hadn't, he suggested, was that innovation and commerce sat uneasily with the established power, and authority, of the Qing dynasty.

Nevertheless, China was changing even if not at the pace of the industrialising west. By the end of the eighteenth century the Chinese Empire extended to its greatest extent – from Manchuria in the northeast to Xinjiang in the northwest. The population had climbed to some three

---

1 Schurmann, F. and Schell, O., *Imperial China,* Harmondsworth, Penguin Books, 1967, 102.

2 Hume, D., *Essays; Moral Political and Literary,* Edinburgh, James Clarke, 1809, Vol. 1, 126.

hundred and thirty million more than double what it had been a hundred and fifty years before. Food production rose and new crops were introduced; roads were made and repaired; the economy flourished. But shadows were beginning to fall over what looked to be a prosperous and secure future. A bigger population increased vulnerability to food shortages and famine; new conquests were expensive to administer and defend; local administration became lax, fuelling impatience with corruption and, later, encouraging rebellion. Perhaps, more worrying and sinister, foreigners were pressing for more structured trading arrangements – and the Qing were becoming increasingly dependent on a steady flow of foreign earnings.

Whilst significant numbers of Scots were involved with China, in differing capacities, from the late eighteenth century, it would be misleading to claim that a "Scottish" connection arose just because an individual had been born, brought up, or educated in Scotland, and lived or worked in China, or *vice versa*. Many Scots came to be in China through employment in British organisations and companies, forging as much a "British" as a "Scottish" connection. But the nature of these encounters, and interactions, was different in context and outcome, and often reflected clearly Scottish derived factors such as the influence of the rational thinking, and utilitarianism, of the Scottish Enlightenment, a strong, democratic, religious tradition, as well as a passion for education. Acute individualism, an independent attitude of mind, and a hard headed business sense, were also part of the mix which more often than not marked out the Scots in China, as elsewhere. A spirit of adventure, and curiosity about a unique and ancient civilization, no doubt, played its part as well. In parallel, growing trade and contact with the west encouraged a small group of Chinese émigrés and students to make their way to Europe, indeed Scotland, in search of employment and education.

The factors which influenced Chinese students and others to come to Scotland, or led to the involvement of Scots in China, are as much a part of Scottish history as they are a contribution to the history of modern China. Although generalising about "the Scots" or "the Chinese" poses the danger of homogenizing different narratives and perceptions, a variety of voices emerge to provide a rich texture of intercultural engagement, even if that process was often demanding, and perplexing, to all involved at the time.

Whether Chinese or Scots they were a disparate, if eclectic, group. Here were businessmen, opium traders and travellers; saints, students and scholars. At once arrogant, greedy and racist, they could be humble, compassionate and kind. In a period of unprecedented change, their lives came together as China emerged slowly, and painfully, to confront, not just the demons from its own past, but the real challenges from beyond its borders, which threatened the very survival of a Chinese identity and, even, of China itself.

This is their remarkable story.

2 Foreign Mud

Nobody will laugh long who deals
much with opium.

THOMAS DE QUINCEY.

Although they were born almost a generation apart, George Bogle and William Jardine shared more than a common Scots tongue. Both came from ambitious families who were anxious to exploit the business and personal opportunities an expanding British Empire offered. Both engaged with China at a time when the Qing Court was beginning to ponder how best to deal with the commercial demands and political challenges posed by people from the west.

Born near Glasgow in 1745, George Bogle studied at Edinburgh University before moving to London where, in 1770, his family contacts secured him a position as a writer (clerk) with the EIC. He was not alone in finding such employment. English attempts to keep the Scots sweet at home resulted in large numbers of them being appointed to posts abroad, particularly in Bengal, where they formed a lively expatriate community in Kolkata. Their interests and influence spread across the subcontinent. Of the eleven trading houses which founded the Mumbai Chamber of Commerce in 1835, nine were owned by Scots.[3]

---

3 Jones, S., *Two Centuries of Overseas Trading; the Origins and Growth of the Inchcape Group,* London, Macmillan, 1986, 7.

The EIC had been formed in 1599 to break the Dutch monopoly of the spice trade to the East Indies but, throughout the eighteenth century, expanded into a variety of other trading ventures and came to occupy large parts of the Indian subcontinent and elsewhere. Bengal came under Company control in 1757, Singapore in 1819, parts of Myanmar (Burma) in 1826 and of Afghanistan in 1839.

Resourceful hardworking and personable, Bogle soon found himself appointed as private secretary to the Governor-General of India, Warren Hastings. When the opportunity arose in 1774, he was the logical choice to lead an exploratory mission to Tibet by way of Bhutan. The EIC's Directors in London hoped the mission would provide more information on Tibet's economy and politics as well as a possible market for the Company's products. Establishing longer term access to China through an overland trading route via Tibet was also an alluring possibility.

Bogle never got to China but he did get to Shigatse in southern Tibet in 1774 accompanied by his Scottish surgeon friend Alexander Hamilton. He was to spend over six months there at the spectacular Tashilhunpo monastery, much of the time in the company of Palden Yeshe, the third Panchen Lama of Tibet.[4] As they both spoke Hindi, they were able to communicate easily – despite Bogle's pronounced Scottish burr - and became good friends.

Although he noted carefully everything he encountered, he remembered most the dreamlike quality of his life at that time. "The novelty of the scenes, and the people I have met with and the ... life I have led, seem a perfect illusion."[5] Whilst there he sought to reassure the Panchen Lama that the EIC was only interested in trade and that Britain had no imperial ambitions regarding Tibet. From memory, he wrote for him a history of Europe and even a (fairly awful) play about the British theatre.

Possibly foreshadowing the Great Game a century later, he learnt from the Panchen Lama about Sino-Russian rivalries along their common

---

4 After the Dalai Lama, the Panchen Lama is the highest ranking Lama in the Gelugpa sect of Tibetan Buddhism. This sect ruled western Tibet from the 16th century until 1951.

5 Markham, C. R., *Narratives of the Mission of George Bogle to Tibet and of the Journey of Thomas Manning to Lhasa*, London, Trubner and Co., 1876, 177.

border and in Mongolia and of Tibetan concerns about maintaining the integrity of their own territory. He obtained a detailed map of Tibet, and information about the country's laws and customs. As to trade, however, the Panchen Lama could do no more than say he would try to promote, in Lhasa and Beijing, the EIC's interest in developing trading relations with Tibet.

Bogle returned safely to Kolkata and was able to fulfil the Panchen Lama's wish that a Buddhist temple be established on the banks of the Ganges near the EIC's headquarters. Bogle died a few years later in 1781, probably of cholera. The Panchen Lama predeceased him the year before, having succumbed to smallpox in Beijing. It seems he was very close to obtaining a passport from the Qianlong Emperor to allow his faraway Scottish friend to visit China's capital.[6] How different might have been future Sino-British relations if he had!

Reflecting the openness of Scottish Enlightenment thinking, and the curiosity of a Himalayan Buddhist court, the exchange between the two men seems to have been warm and genuine, and provides a unique insight into Tibetan life, and the thinking of an itinerant Scotsman, at the end of the eighteenth century. Aside from its own intrinsic interest, Bogle's mission remains important today since the Chinese claim it implies Britain recognised Chinese sovereignty over Tibet.

Despite Bogle's efforts, however, China continued to be an attractive, if distant, market in the eighteenth century, largely because there was no demand for British manufactured goods. This situation was exacerbated when tea drinking became popular, not just among the habitués of London's coffee houses, but with people across much of Britain. By 1750, the EIC was importing nearly two and a half million kilos of tea each year and paying for it all in silver.

How was this trade to be financed if the Chinese were unwilling to purchase British goods? The EIC saw its opportunity. The sale of opium had been banned in China since 1729, but demand for the narcotic was booming. What better way to redress the trade deficit than through the sale of opium in China. Holding a monopoly on its sale in India, the EIC encouraged the cultivation of opium in Bengal but, to circumvent

---

6 Teltscher, K., *The High Road to China,* London, Bloomsbury, 2006, 223-24.

the 1729 ban, did not ship it directly to China. Instead, it was sold to American, British and Indian traders who, on reaching the China coast, sold the opium on to local smugglers for silver. These traders then sold the silver back to the EIC for bills of exchange payable in India, or London. The silver funded the EIC's purchase of tea. Very quickly, the trade balance was reversed in Britain's favour because more opium was being imported into China than tea and silk exported to the west. The Chinese referred disparagingly to imported opium as "foreign mud".

When the EIC's monopoly on trade with China was revoked by the British Parliament in 1834, traders like William Jardine sought to fill the vacuum and strengthen their own position as leaders in the highly lucrative China market. Riches few might dream of were within the grasp of those willing to risk their all in the narcotics trade. When he died in 1843, Jardine was one of the wealthiest men in Britain having amassed his fortune though a mix of commercial dexterity, political sensitivity and luck.

Jardine came from a family who farmed near Lochmaben in Dumfriesshire. Like many young men from that area, then and since, he studied at Edinburgh, completing his studies in medicine in 1802. Edinburgh's prestigious medical schools were renowned for training innovative medical practitioners who readily found employment in the EIC as ships surgeons. Aged just eighteen, Jardine sailed as a surgeon's mate on the *Brunswick* for China. It was to be a connection that lasted throughout his lifetime and was extended subsequently by his descendants.

Jardine's career typifies that of many Scots who sought fame and fortune in nineteenth century China - even if many of them were not as successful. Known to the Chinese as "iron headed old rat" he moved on from surgery to concentrate on fashioning a series of commercial alliances which resulted in the formation of Jardine Matheson & Company in 1832.[7] Jardine's principal partner was another Scot, James Matheson, from Lairg in Sutherland, who had likewise been educated at Edinburgh. Through family connections, Matheson had made his way to China by way of Kolkata.

---

7 The Company was known in Chinese by the auspicious name of *Ewo* meaning *Happy Harmony.*

Since 1757, China's legal foreign trade had been managed by a small number of Chinese firms, known as the *cohong*, (combined merchant companies), based in Guangzhou (Canton) where foreign traders were allowed to visit during the trading season between October and March – the largest group were the British, many of them Scots. Trading was not allowed anywhere else along the south China coast. In exchange for a trading monopoly, the *cohong* was expected to supervise their foreign trading partners and ensure compliance with local regulations and customs – not always an easy task!

These cumbersome arrangements frustrated the ambitions of men like Jardine and Matheson who were anxious to open up further trading opportunities with China. So was the EIC which had earlier sent a well-placed young Scot, Hugh H. Lindsay, on a secret reconnaissance mission to ascertain the practicality of trading direct with ports other than Guangzhou.[8] An agenda was clearly being formulated for future expansion. William John Napier, 9th Lord Napier of Merchiston, was sent by the British Government to Guangzhou in 1834 to attempt to negotiate better trading terns for British merchants. His mission was unsuccessful and he died in Macau in the same year. Nevertheless, wherever trading took place, its financial viability turned on the continued import into China of large volumes of opium which was becoming increasingly unacceptable to the Court in Beijing. Partially to restrict the outflow of silver, and to combat the debilitating effects of opium use, the Chinese started to crack down on the narcotics trade.

When the Imperial Commissioner, Lin Zexu, tried to suppress the expanding opium trade in Guangzhou in 1839, destroying over twenty one thousand, three hundred chests of opium, hostilities quickly followed. Because of superior western firepower, the outcome was inevitable. With the British in possession of Shanghai and Zhenjiang (Jingjiang), and their gunboats in control of the Yangzi, the Chinese were forced, by the Treaty of Nanjing (Nanking) in 1842, to agree humiliating terms which included opening the five coastal ports of Guangzhou, Xiamen

---

8 Lindsay's father was a younger brother of Alexander Lindsay, 6th Earl of Balcarres and a Director of the EIC. For details of Lindsay's voyage see *The Secret Mission of the Lord Amherst on the China Coast, 1832* in Hsu, I. C.Y., *Harvard Journal of Asiatic Studies,* Harvard, Harvard-Yenching Institute, 1954, Vol. 17, No. 1/2, 231-52.

(Amoy), Fuzhou (Foochow), Ningbo (Ningpo) and Shanghai to trade and residence by British consuls and traders. In what were to become known as the "treaty ports", British residents were placed in an extra-territorial position, such that they were excluded from the jurisdiction of Chinese officials, and the Chinese legal system, and made subject to British courts, and English law.

More importantly, the Chinese agreed that the barren, rocky island of Hong Kong, with its wonderful natural harbour at the mouth of the Pearl River, should come under direct British control. Extended to include the Kowloon peninsula in 1860, and the adjacent "new" territories leased for ninety nine years in 1898, the British crown colony of Hong Kong was to become, eventually, one of the leading western commercial centres on the China coast.

Poor harvests, corrupt officials and increased taxation fuelled rebellion and civil discord across much of southern China in the 1840s and '50s. Believing he was God's second son, a village schoolmaster, Hong Xiuquan, organised his followers into an army and headed north for Beijing. He called his movement the Heavenly Kingdom of Universal Peace (Taiping). The Taiping revolutionaries nearly toppled the Qing dynasty and were only finally defeated in 1864 after the staggering loss of over twenty million lives.

For the western powers, the on-going political instability provided an opportunity to increase their trading and diplomatic demands on the beleaguered Court in Beijing. Britain proposed that the 1842 Treaty of Nanjing be renegotiated to allow the opening of more ports on the coast and inland towns, the abolition of tariffs, and the legalising of the opium trade. When these demands were rejected, an Anglo-French army attacked first Guangzhou and eventually Beijing where the Summer Palace (Yihe Yuan) and the Old Summer Palace (Yuan Ming Yuan) were looted and destroyed. As High Commissioner and plenipotentiary in China and the Far East, it was a Scot, James Bruce, 8th Earl of Elgin and 12th Earl of Kincardine, who presided over the destruction of the palaces. He believed this wanton destruction "would produce a greater effect in China, and on the emperor, than persons at a distance may suppose."[9] One of the worst acts of vandalism in modern times, many of

---

9 Hevia, J. L., *English Lessons; The Pedagogy of Imperialism in Nineteenth-Century China,* Durham NC, Duke University Press, 2003, 106.

the treasures of the palaces were looted and sold by auction in London and elsewhere, or remain in regimental museums in Britain.

The 1860 Convention of Beijing, which concluded the hostilities, saw all of the allies aims achieved, including legalising of the opium trade, freedom of travel to inland areas, and freedom of religion. Eleven more ports were opened to foreign trade, where British residents were to enjoy extraterritorial rights, and British, and other commercial vessels, allowed to sail on the Yangzi River from Shanghai into the heart of the country. China's humiliation was complete.

After 1860, the Yangzi was patrolled by Royal Navy gunboats operating out of Hankou (Hankow) in Hubei Province. Many of these vessels, like HMS *Sandpiper* and HMS *Cricket,* were built on the Clyde by companies such as Yarrows and Barclay Curle, whilst some of the smaller ones, like HMS *Bee,* were fabricated at the Ailsa Shipbuilding Company in Troon. The smaller vessels were usually shipped to China and assembled there; the larger vessels were towed from the Clyde to the China coast. The Royal Navy's China Station not only demonstrated Britain's new found power and prestige but served the very practical purpose of providing protection for British vessels on the Yangzi and the other great rivers of China - the Yellow River to the north, and the Pearl River in the south.

British and other western firms moved quickly to exploit the new trading opportunities now available with the opening up of the longest river in Asia. Two Scottish controlled companies led the way – first Jardine Matheson & Co. and then Lindsay & Co. So proactive were they that, within a generation, the Yangzi valley became effectively a British sphere of influence from which other foreign competitors were excluded.[10]

Jardine Matheson's office in Shanghai, opened by Alexander Dallas from Inverness in 1844, provided a base for operations in the Yangzi. The tea and silk trade prospered as did the export of Chinese cotton to Europe to meet the shortage caused by the American civil war. The import of opium also continued until increasing competition from Chinese

---

10 The British sphere of influence in the Yangzi valley was formalised in an Anglo-Chinese treaty of February 1898.

grown opium, and from other buyers in India, forced Jardine Matheson to pull out of the narcotics business completely in 1872.

Jardine Matheson was not the only British company involved in trade in China in these years. Until their bankruptcy in 1865 and 1867 respectively, Lindsay & Co., and the mighty Dent & Co., were major players aggressively pushing their interests along the south China coast and in the Yangzi. So too was Gibb Livingston & Co. founded in 1836 in Guangzhou by two Scots, Thomas Augustus Gibb and William Potter Livingston. Whilst new companies like Butterfield & Swire came on the scene, Jardine Matheson managed to hold on to its dominant position as "the princely hong" largely due to a succession of remarkable Scots, like William Keswick, who guided the company and diversified its interests through challenging times.

Grandson of Jean Johnstone, William Jardine's elder sister, William Keswick first went to China in 1855, becoming a partner in Jardine Matheson seven years later after setting up the company's operations in Japan. Over the next hundred and fifty years, five further generations of Keswicks were to continue the family connection with the company. What did they have in common? Almost all of them came from southern Scotland to where most of them returned having made their fortune in China and elsewhere in Asia.

Like so many other Scots abroad in the nineteenth and early twentieth centuries, they ran a close knit family business, depending, in the main, on family contacts and connections to manage their far flung interests. They also shared common values including ambition, determination, loyalty and thrift which had been forged in the educational and religious framework of the Scotland of their day. All these qualities were to come into play in the scramble for business along the Yangzi ` and beyond.

The development of railways in China, seen by all the foreign powers as essential for economic growth, opened up opportunities for Scottish engineers as well as for the export from Scotland of railway engines and rolling stock. The British obtained more miles of railway concessions than any other nation, entrusting their development to the aggressive British and Chinese Corporation formed in 1898 to promote British commercial

Critical to the development of railways, as well as other infrastructure, was ready access to capital in what was thought to be a fickle, but potentially lucrative, market. Here again Scots played a major role in establishing and managing, financial institutions which sought to meet the needs of China's growing economy.

Through family connections, Thomas Sutherland from Aberdeen had been fortunate to secure appointment as a clerk with the Peninsular & Oriental Company (P&O) in London from where he progressed, via Mumbai, to Hong Kong. There he became Superintendent of P&O's operations in China and Japan. Already a successful entrepreneur, he went on in 1863 to become the first chairman of the Hong Kong and Whampoa Dock Company which provided facilities for the Royal Navy as well as serving commercial interests in the region. More importantly, he identified the need for "a bank in China more or less founded upon Scottish principles" which would facilitate trade with China, and the development of a modern infrastructure. What he envisaged was a joint stock company trading as an issuing bank through a branch network as had been the practice in Scotland prior to the 1845 Banking Act. Clearly, the fledgling colony of Hong Kong had neither the capacity nor the resources to establish or manage an issuing bank. Moreover, Indian based investors were keen to set up a financial institution over which local traders would have little control. Sutherland moved quickly. With the support of fellow Scots, like William Adamson of the Borneo Company, and other China based investors, the doors of the Hongkong and Shanghai Bank were opened for business in 1864; "the Bank" as it became known throughout China was incorporated in Hong Kong two years later. Sutherland was its first Vice Chairman.

Scots were actively involved in the development and operation of the Bank from its early days. Harry Panmure Gordon from Perthshire acted as the Bank's agent in the City of London arranging loan finance. After a varied banking career in Scotland, India, China and Japan, Ewen Cameron from Culloden near Inverness became the Bank's highly effective senior manager in London. Initially reluctant to become involved, Jardine Matheson worked with the Bank from 1898 onwards through the British and Chinese Corporation – its senior directors were William Keswick of Jardine Matheson and Ewen Cameron of the Bank.[14] Other Scots followed. The son of a Free Church Minister educated at Edinburgh Academy and Edinburgh University, Charles Stewart Addis is remembered for his work on the 1913 Reorganisation Loan of £25 million to China when he persuaded national banking syndicates to work together, rather than compete with each other, to meet better perceived Chinese needs. He later served on the China Famine Relief Committee and other organizations focused on the development of the Chinese economy. Renowned for its prudence, the Bank always exuded a Scots ethos and provided opportunities for Scots like Willie Purves from Kelso who, in 1992, became the first chairman of the holding company for the Bank.

Scots involvement in banking in China was not restricted, however, only to the Hongkong Bank. Founder of *The Economist* newspaper, James Wilson from Hawick promoted the formation of the Chartered Bank of India, Australia and China. Granted a Royal Charter in 1853, it opened its first office in Hong Kong in 1859 and is Hong Kong's oldest bank.

In addition to trade and banking, Scots business involvement in China extended to a variety of other activities including bookselling, journalism and retailing. One of China's most famous English language publishers and retailers was established in 1876 when the Irish printer, Kelly, teamed up with the Scots bookseller, Walsh, to provide a bookshop on the bund in Shanghai. The company published a range of books mostly on Asian history and culture.

They certainly would have stocked the travel and political writings of Alexander Michie, the son of a sailor from Earlsferry in Fife who came to Hong Kong when he was only nineteen. Five years later he was appointed a partner with Lindsay & Co., and sent as their representative to Shanghai. He held appointments with a number of firms before working as Jardine Matheson's agent in Tianjin. Like many of his countrymen, he took an active part in expatriate community life in Shanghai. He served as a Municipal Councillor, on the Committee of the North China Branch of the Royal Asiatic Society and on the local Chamber of Commerce.

---

14 Ewen Cameron's son was British Prime Minister David Cameron's great grandfather.

What distinguishes Michie, however, is that from 1886 to 1891 he edited the *Chinese Times,* the aim of which was to spread "information about foreign countries among the Chinese and about China to foreigners". But like so many of his generation he believed that China was on the point of disintegration. "Having no guiding principles ... there remains nothing for China but to be squeezed into such shape as the hard bodies she meets with determine. Other hands must mould her, since she is not capable of moulding herself."[15] He wrote extensively on Chinese issues and authored *The Siberian overland route from Peking to Petersburg,* a charming narrative about his fellow countryman, John Bell of Antermony near Glasgow who travelled from Russia to China in 1720 – probably the first Scot to visit Beijing.

Others had more faith than Michie in the future of China. Two young Scots, Thomas Lane and Ninian Crawford, set up in business in Hong Kong as ships' chandlers in 1850 in a makeshift bamboo hut. They later expanded into the bakery business to be able to provide ships biscuits for the vessels they serviced. Shrewd and hardworking, their store became, and remains, one of Hong Kong's leading department stores, Lane Crawford. The company also operates a store in Beijing and in the past had stores in Guangzhou, Shanghai and Kobe and Tokyo in Japan.

There were opportunities too for people with professional expertise and finance. Trained in medicine at Edinburgh University, Dr. Thomas Boswell Watson from Haddington practised first in Macau before moving to Hong Kong where he acquired an interest in the Hong Kong Dispensary known locally as the "Big Medicine Shop". Just prior to his return to Scotland in 1859, Dr Watson was joined by his nephew, Dr Alexander Skirving Watson, who assumed responsibility for the dispensing side of the business. Named after him, Watsons the Chemist developed an extensive branch network in Hong Kong.[16]

Another Scot, Alexander Findlay Smith who had once worked for the Highland Railway, proposed and supervised the construction of Asia's first able funicular railway which ran from the central business district

---

15 Cannon, I. D., *Public success, private sorrow; the life and times of Charles Henry Brewitt-Taylor (1857-1938),* Hong Kong, Hong Kong University Press, 2009, 192.

16 Waters, D. in *Journal of the Royal Asiatic Society, Hong Kong Branch,* Vol. 30 (1990), Hong Kong, Royal Asiatic Society, Hong Kong Branch, 238-39.

through Victoria Gap to the Peak in Hong Kong some five hundred and fifty metres above sea level. Opened in 1888, the Peak Tram facilitated residential development in the cooler Peak area of Hong Kong Island. Today it is a major tourist attraction carrying over four million people each year to enjoy the spectacular views. Perhaps men like Watson and Smith were fortunate to be based in the comparatively stable society of Hong Kong even if its bland British overlay of justice and freedom masked notions of racial superiority and condescension towards Chinese people.

Other Scots seized the business opportunities China offered. In 1862 John Macgregor and Jack Caldbeck bought over a small business in Shanghai specialising in the import of wine and spirits. By the end of the century they had branches along the China coast as well as in Beijing and Tianjin becoming one of the best known liquor retailers in Asia. They pioneered a sale or return approach to the wine and spirit trade which was popular with clubs, hotels and messes.[17] A different type of drink was pioneered by Dr (later Sir) Patrick Manson who established the Dairy Farm Company in 1886 to provide a hygienic milk supply in Hong Kong. From 1890 until 1920 the herd was managed by a Scottish farmer, James Walker.

Scots continued to play an important role in business in China throughout the first half of the twentieth century facing the challenges of economic downturn, invasion, rebellion and war. The nascent nationalist movement, particularly after the May Thirtieth Incident in 1925, organized repeated boycotts of British goods. Moreover, Chinese companies were starting to deal directly with foreign companies, thereby side-lining the role of the established agency houses like Jardine Matheson and Swire. To survive and prosper, what was required was not just a new business model but a new approach to Chinese staff and customers which saw them as stakeholders in business enterprise and success rather than grateful recipients of British largesse. The manager of Swire's Shanghai operations in the 1920s and '30s, N. S. Brown from Glasgow, played a pivotal role in pushing through long overdue attitudinal changes which transformed Swire's management. Similar moves followed in other companies. The treaty port community, however, was less enthusiastic

---

17 Jones, *op. cit.*, 187-88.

as many expatriates were now required to deal with Chinese as equals rather than subordinates – not for nothing was Brown often referred to by many of his staff as "Night Soil Brown"![18]

Following the revolution in 1949 virtually all foreign owned businesses were nationalised though some sought refuge in Hong Kong from where they continued to trade. Although new China's fragile economy faced overwhelming challenges, and the longer term outlook was uncertain, trade and business did expand though in ways very different from the past. No longer would overseas businesses secure advantageous trading positions because of their support and endorsement of, western political objectives. And never again would there be foreign mud on the coast or elsewhere in China.

---

18 Winchester, S., *The River at the Centre of the World*, London, Penguin, 1998, 2.

3 An Open Door that No One Can Shut

China for Christ in this generation.
Why not?

J. C. GARRITT.

The first to be led out was George Farthing of the Baptist Mission. Although his wife clung to him, he gently put her aside and, going in front of the soldiers, knelt down without a word - his head was struck off by one blow of the executioner's knife. He was quickly followed by three of his colleagues, and the young medical missionary, Dr. William Millar Wilson from Glasgow, who was likewise beheaded. As the slaughter continued one of the women pleaded "We all came to China to bring you the good news of the salvation by Jesus Christ; we have done you no harm, only good, why do you treat us so?" Her call for mercy was to no avail. She and the other women were beheaded as were their terrified children – their bodies being thrown outside the city wall for the scavenging dogs.[19]

Perhaps those killed that day in 1900 at Taiyuan in Shanxi Province were fortunate. Elsewhere missionaries and their families were subjected to horrific torture and cruelty. A few made it to cities on the coast after perilous journeys when they were attacked and stoned. Foreigners

---

19 Preston, D., *The Boxer Rebellion*, New York, Walker & Company, 1999, 279-81.

in Beijing were under siege as well. Western intervention in China and hopes of Christianising the country clearly faced serious challenges.

China's defeat by emergent Japan in 1895 had been seen as a national humiliation and, possibly, the prelude to the partition of the country by other nations. Anti-foreign sentiment, fuelled by poverty and fanned by conservative elements at the Qing Court, spread rapidly throughout the country finding a local focus in western missionaries who were often living in remote, inaccessible locations. They were visible and vulnerable.

Who were these apparently heartless murderers? Disparagingly referred to by foreigners as "Boxers", because of their martial arts and callisthenics routines, the Righteous Harmony Society spread rapidly from Shandong Province throughout much of northern China in the closing years of the nineteenth century. Comprised largely of peasants, it was mystical, nationalistic and virulently anti-Christian. The Boxers believed they were immune from injury and could call in aid spirit soldiers who would help them cleanse China of foreign influences.[20] Although the rebellion was eventually repressed, following the intervention of the western powers and Japan, the Boxers articulated widespread concerns about the integrity of China itself that were to echo down the new century right through to the revolution of 1949.

The Protestant missionary movement in China grew out of the eighteenth century evangelical revival which was, itself, a reaction to the rationalism of the Enlightenment and an attempt to reclaim those being lost to Christianity through rapid industrialisation and urbanisation. John Wesley and later William Wilberforce placed great emphasis on piety, bible study and personal conversion. Their burning interest in contemporary humanitarian issues, including education for the poor and the abolition of slavery, quickly extended to bringing Christ's gospel to areas coming under British control or informal influence.

After the defeat of France in 1814, the balance of power in the west moved in Britain's favour, ensuring that British economic interests and political clout would prevail throughout the century that followed. Control of the seas by the Royal Navy hastened the process of finding

20 Preston, *op. cit.*, Prologue.

outlets for new manufacturing processes, and the raw materials that fed them, and provided opportunities to make financial profit as well as to save souls.

What became known as the Baptist Missionary Society (BMS) was formed in 1792 and the Church Missionary Society (CMS) in 1799.[21] From the start many missions were interdenominational in focus like the London Missionary Society (LMS) inaugurated in 1795, and the Scottish Society, later known as the Scottish Missionary Society, which was founded the following year. "I have placed before you an open door that no one can shut" was an appropriate tract for the times.[22]

Between 1800 and 1950 Scottish Protestant missionary involvement with China falls into four phases each of which was shaped by different religious and political factors. Initially, because of the restraints on residence which confined missionaries to the Portuguese enclave of Macau, and to Guangzhou, the focus was on translating the scriptures into Chinese and providing study aids, such as Chinese dictionaries, for use by missionaries and other foreigners. Opportunities for direct missionary work were limited. However, following the end of the first Anglo-Chinese War, the 1842 Treaty of Nanjing, which guaranteed the rights of foreigners in the five "treaty ports", nudged open the door for those seeking to harvest souls along the China coast.

Missionaries now had a firmer footing but progress was slow. However, it was not until after the second Anglo-Chinese War nearly twenty years later that Europeans gained almost unimpeded access to the interior of China and guarantees for the security of Chinese converts.[23] The China Inland Mission (CIM) was formed in 1865 - the future looked bright.

Throughout the remainder of the nineteenth century Protestant missions sought to expand their influence in new areas of outreach whilst consolidating their hold in the cities along the coast where they could count on a small, if growing, number of supporters.

---

21 Stanley, B., *The History of the Baptist Missionary Society 1792 -1992*, Edinburgh, T. & T. Clark, 1992, 20-22.

22 *The Bible,* Revelation 3:8, New International Version, 1984.

23 The Treaty of Tianjin (Tientsin) 1858 and the Convention of Beijing 1860.

British Protestant engagement at this time was not without its difficulties and dilemmas. What was an appropriate response to the Taiping revolutionaries with their emphasis on elements of Christianity? Should they be supported despite their theological peculiarities and the humanitarian disaster their civil war precipitated? Moreover, were missionaries compromised by their close association with British trade and imperialism? Was the humiliation of China in the two Anglo-Chinese wars a sound foundation from which to proclaim the love of Christ? How were young churches to grow? Was it better to seek the conversion of large numbers of poor peasants, dismissively referred to as "rice Christians", or target the scholarly gentleman class?

Despite the doubts raised, and difficulties posed, by the Boxer rising, and its aftermath, the number of Protestant missionaries serving around the country increased after 1900 to some eight thousand, including support workers.[24] Although by the 1920s Protestant missions claimed over half a million adherents, educated Chinese church leaders were almost non-existent and missionary endeavours remained very much foreign controlled in structure and outlook. Nevertheless, there was a growing conviction, articulated at the 1907 Centenary Missionary Conference in Shanghai and, later, at the World Missionary Conference at Edinburgh in 1910, that China, indeed the world, could be evangelised within a generation. These Conferences met during a time of unprecedented change and uncertainty in China which saw the death of the Empress Dowager in 1908 followed by the collapse of dynasty itself and the formation of the Republic in 1911.

Whilst missions came to play a significant role in Chinese modernisation, and promoted Western style education, which was embraced enthusiastically by reformers like Zhang Zhidong, unease about foreign involvement, of whatever kind, was never far below the surface. Many young people were impatient with the pace of reform, concerned about the lawlessness, and anarchy, that prevailed across much of China and suspicious that westerners, including missionaries, were taking advantage of China's weakness.

On 30 May 1925, when British officered police fired on demonstrators in Shanghai, killing nine and injuring many others, riots followed.

---

24 Stanley, B., *The Bible and the Flag*, London, Apollos, 1990, 140.

Anti-foreign disturbances also took place in Nanjing two years later when six westerners were killed and thousands of missionaries fled the country. Almost too late, many of them began to realise that nationalism was a real force, and that urgent steps needed to be taken to establish churches that were truly autonomous and not closely associated with western identities and values.

The new China that was then emerging was very different from that which Robert Morrison first encountered when he came to Macau in September 1807. Today, the waterfront at Macau is home to high rise buildings and casinos which overlook quaint churches, pretty houses and quiet gardens. Tourists come in their thousands to try their luck at the casinos which surpass those of Las Vegas in turnover and opulence.

Then, Macau was a bustling seaport and shipbuilding centre and the focus of Europe's trade with China. In the crowded, narrow alleys, the Portuguese rubbed shoulders with Americans, Chinese, Danes and Germans. Of course, the British were there as well with the EIC having the most prestigious premises on the Praia Grande. And it was his appointment as a translator for that company which provided Morrison with the resources that allowed him to pursue his missionary work in Macau and Guangzhou. Apart from a three year furlough in Britain, Morrison was to spend the remaining twenty seven years of his life in China. He had no illusions as to the challenges he faced. Shortly before his arrival he was asked whether he expected to have any spiritual impact on the Chinese. "No sir" he replied," but I expect God will!"[25]

The son of a Scottish farm labourer, Morrison joined the LMS in 1804 but was uncertain where he might serve. His decision to become a missionary in China was influenced by another Scotsman, David Bogue from Coldingham, who was then ministering at the Congregational Church at Gosport in Hampshire and providing further training for LMS recruits before they went abroad.

Faith and conviction certainly played their part in Morrison's life – luck did as well. A chance encounter in London in 1805 led him to meet Yong Sam-tak a student from Guangzhou. They quickly agreed to swop

---

25 Tucker, R. A., *From Jerusalem to Irian Jaya; a biographical history of Christian Missions*, Grand Rapids, Michigan, Zondervan, 2nd. Ed., 2004, 178.

English for Chinese tuition. From Yong Morrison obtained his first insights into the Chinese language. He also learnt, as his wife remembered, something of the problems he might encounter in the future as Yong told him that "my country not custom to talky of God's business"![26] They studied an anonymous translation of the Gospels, probably made by a Jesuit missionary, which had been found in the British Library. With Yong's assistance, Morrison transcribed the document as well as a hand written Latin–Chinese dictionary. As his linguistic skills improved, he decided it was time to set out on his great adventure. He was ordained at the Scotch Kirk on Swallow Street in London early in January 1807 and set sail for China, via the United States, later that month.

Like missionaries in China and elsewhere, Morrison came to realise very quickly that the threats posed by other Christians were often more dangerous than those emanating from potential converts. He was able to stay in Macau for only three days before being expelled as the Roman Catholic priests there bitterly opposed the arrival of a Protestant missionary. His early years in China were besought with difficulties. He was robbed, cheated and humiliated but he persevered with his translation work. Assisted by another Scot, William Milne, Morrison completed his translation of the Bible in 1819; his Dictionary of the Chinese Language was printed in 1823.[27]

Morrison's role in the advance of Christianity in China stands almost without parallel. Although he is remembered for his pioneering scholarly work, and his role in establishing the Anglo-Chinese College in Malacca at the southern end of the Malay peninsula (it was relocated to Hong Kong in 1843), he drew, perhaps, the greatest personal satisfaction from the baptism in 1814 "at a spring of water issuing from the foot of a lofty hill by the sea side, away from human observation" of one of his assistants, Tsae A-Ko, the first Protestant Chinese Christian.[28] However, the antagonism shown against those Chinese who converted

---

26 Morrison, E., *Memoirs of the Life and Labours of Robert Morrison*, London, Longman, Orme, Brown, Green, 1839, Vol. 1, 80.

27 Hancock, C., *Robert Morrison and the Birth of Chinese Protestantism*, London, T. & T. Clark, 2008, 128.

28 Hancock, *op. cit.,* 111.

to Christianity was to haunt the missionary movement throughout the century that followed.

Whilst Morrison's application and zeal came from his strong personal faith, he also acknowledged the importance education had upon shaping his life and defining his work. Like so many of his countrymen, education was perceived as being important to the evolution of a Christian society, whether that be in China or Scotland which, by the early 18th century, boasted a functioning national education system unparalleled elsewhere in Europe since classical times. With its emphasis on first principles and philosophy, Scottish education was to impact on the structure and curriculum of evolving Chinese schools and colleges as well as influencing the thinking of many missionaries coming to China.

One such missionary was Morrison's intellectual successor, James Legge, from Huntly in Aberdeenshire. His first appointment overseas as an LMS missionary was as Head Master of Ying Wa College which Morrison had earlier founded – he held that post for nearly thirty years.

Legge is remembered as one of the foremost British sinologists of the nineteenth century believing that, if he was to understand the thinking of potential converts, he would first have to understand their culture and values. Towards this end, he started in 1841 to translate the Chinese canonical texts, including the principal works of Confucius, an enormous task that took many years to complete. Although some of the translation techniques Legge used are now outdated, much of his work remains without parallel today. For his outstanding contribution to scholarship, Legge was appointed in 1876 the first Professor of Chinese Language and Literature at Oxford, a post he held until his death in 1897.

In seeking to understand the Chinese mind, Legge brought to his commentaries, and translation work, a balanced religious and philosophical worldview which owed much both to his upbringing in a dissenting family and his education. Studying at Aberdeen Grammar School, and at King's College in Aberdeen, he embraced the thinking of Scottish Enlightenment figures like Dugald Stewart and Francis Hutcheson with their emphasis on tolerance and rationality. Stewart's conciliatory views were readily absorbed and formed the basis for both respecting and trying to understand different beliefs.

Scottish education also played a significant role in other areas of missionary endeavour in China, particularly as regards medical care and research. The international influence of Scottish medicine has long been one of its distinguishing features. The interface which developed between medical education in Scotland and the overseas world was vibrant and multifaceted. This is particularly evident during the nineteenth century when British expansion overseas provided new areas of influence for Scotland's medical schools, and enhanced opportunities for students from abroad to study medicine in Scotland. Awareness of the educational challenges, and professional medical opportunities which arose, hastened the engagement of Scottish trained doctors with the health care needs of evolving communities abroad. Their contribution to global health care during this period was outstanding and completely out of proportion to their numbers. They were renowned around the world for their clinical and research skill, as well as their determination – China was to be no exception.

Patrick Manson's ground-breaking contribution to medical research and education in China was not just of national importance but had an international dimension as well because of his insight into the role of mosquitoes in spreading malaria, and his pioneering work in the development of tropical medicine as a discreet discipline. Educated at Aberdeen University, he first came to China in 1866 as an employee of the Chinese Imperial Maritime Customs, serving in Taiwan and Xiamen. Later relocating to Hong Kong, he was the driving force behind the establishment of the Hong Kong College of Medicine for Chinese in 1887 which was later to form the nucleus of the Medical Faculty of Hong Kong University. Subsequently appointed Chief Medical Officer at the British Colonial Office, Manson championed the establishment of training facilities for tropical medicine. The London School of Hygiene and Tropical Medicine was opened in 1899; a lectureship in tropical medicine had been established at Edinburgh in the previous year.

From the beginning of the nineteenth Century, Scottish medical missionaries were active all over China. Whilst employed by the EIC, Thomas Richardson Colledge opened the first ophthalmic clinic for Chinese in Macau in 1827 and went on to found the Medical Mission Society of

China in 1837.[29] A graduate of Edinburgh University, James Laidlaw Maxwell set up the first Presbyterian Church and medical mission in Taiwan in 1865 whilst serving with the English Presbyterian Mission.[30] Together with other health care professionals, Scottish trained doctors and nurses contributed, not just to the practice of medicine in China, but also to the development of hospitals and other medical institutions as well as the translation into the Chinese language of western medical monographs and literature.

Something of the diversity of medical missionary work in China is captured in the life Dr. D. Duncan Main from Kirkmichael who worked as a medical missionary in Hangzhou from 1881 to 1926. Main remembered the hostility which greeted him and his wife on their arrival, the plight of the lepers and opium addicts and the stench of untreated wounds which cleared the waiting room of patients and almost made him faint. Like many other medical missionaries, he travelled to distant patients which often posed unexpected dangers. On one occasion he strayed into quick sands on the east bank of the Chien Tang River. Not until he had sunk up to his armpits was he rescued by two passing boatmen who heard his cries for help. For men like Main, care of the sick was the top priority but the end-game was conversion of the patient to Christianity. "There is no pulpit so influential as a hospital ward" he once wrote, "and no pew where the hearer is so receptive as a hospital bed ... it is an integral part of ... winning men to Christ."[31]

Medical missionary work was an important, but not the only, aspect of Scottish missionary endeavour in China. Born near Stonehaven in 1861, Moir Duncan came to China in 1888 having undergone an intense conversion whilst a teenager in Glasgow when he resolved to become a missionary in China. Working mainly in remote Shanxi Province for the BMS, Duncan sought to influence local leaders and the intelligentsia rather than the peasantry – a strategy that certainly saved his life as he

---

29 Richardson took an MD from Aberdeen in 1839 and became a Fellow of the Royal College of Physicians of Edinburgh in 1840.

30 His sons John Preston Maxwell, and James Laidlaw Jnr., also served as medical missionaries in China.

31 De Gruche, K., *Dr. D. Duncan Main of Hangchow,* London & Edinburgh, Marshall, Morgan & Scott, 1930, 43 and 160.

was tipped off by the Governor of Shanxi about the dangers posed by the Boxers and was able to flee with his family to safety in Shanghai. After the uprising, his conviction that western learning was critical to the modernisation of China and the advance of Christianity resulted in his appointment in 1906 as the first Principal of what was to become Shanxi University. His untimely death that year of tuberculosis cut short what might have been a significant contribution to higher educational development in China.[32]

By contrast, William Chalmers Burns was one of the leading evangelists of his day who had been at the forefront of a major revival in 1839 at Kilsyth in Lanarkshire where his father was a Church of Scotland minister. He travelled extensively throughout Scotland preaching his message of repentance and salvation as well as visiting Ireland and Canada where he promoted the interests of the newly established Free Church of Scotland. Always attracted to mission work, he was drawn to India but volunteered for service in China with the English Presbyterian Mission in 1847 when he heard of the urgent need for missionaries there.

Dressed in traditional Chinese clothing, Burns travelled extensively throughout southern China. His views on lay evangelism were to have considerable influence on the young William Hudson Taylor whom he first met by chance in Shanghai in 1855 and on the future structure of the CIM which Taylor established subsequently. Years later, Taylor remembered the approach of "this beloved servant of God" to grass roots evangelism -

> *"We were in the habit of leaving our boats, after prayer for blessing, at about nine o'clock in the morning, with a light bamboo stool in hand. Selecting a suitable station, one would mount the stool and speak for twenty minutes, while the other was pleading for blessing; and then changing places, the voice of the first speaker had a rest. After an hour or two thus occupied, we would move on to another point at some distance from the first, and speak again. Usually about midday we returned to our boats for dinner, fellowship, and prayer, and then resumed our out-door work until dusk. After tea and further rest, we would go with our native helpers to some tea-shop, where several hours might be spent in free conversation with the*

---

32 *Biographical Dictionary of Chinese Christianity*, www.bdcconline.net/duncan-moir.

people. Not infrequently before leaving a town we had good reason to believe that much truth had been grasped; and we placed many Scriptures and books in the hands of those interested."[33]

Although it was relentless labour, which would have broken stronger men of less conviction, the pull of missionary service in China remained strong even as the emphasis changed gradually from grass roots evangelism to growing young churches.

The son of a Free Church of Scotland theological professor, John Campbell Gibson made an important contribution to the development of an indigenous Chinese church free from foreign control. Drawing on the thinking of Henry Venn, the missionary strategist who had argued that churches in the mission field should be self-supporting, self-governing, and self-extending, Gibson urged missionaries to remember that they were not "pegging out a claim" on Chinese soil for a western sect. "We are not in China to fit together mechanically a reduced copy of the forms in which the course of history has moulded the Churches of our birth. We are not there to translate into Chinese the Westminster Confession of Faith, or the Thirty-Nine Articles or the Heidelberg Catechism". Missionaries had been properly involved, he said, in the formation of new Churches - but Chinese people needed and wanted freedom to manage the affairs of their own church.[34]

Although his views were widely discussed in the missionary community of the day, it was not really until the more fraught 1920's that they were progressively implemented after the formation of the National Christian Council in 1922 which sought to speed up the localisation of Protestant missions in China. Today, the principles of self-government, financial independence and the evangelisation of Chinese by Chinese form the basis of the Three Self Patriotic Movement, the only state recognised church in the reformed tradition in China.[35]

---

33 Taylor, J.H., *Retrospect,* Toronto, China Inland Mission, 3rd. Ed., 1902, 59-60.

34 Gibson, J.C., *Mission Problems and Mission Methods in South China,* New York Chicago and Toronto, Fleming H. Revell & Co., 1902, 199 and 232.

35 Lian Xi, *Redeemed by Fire - The Rise of Popular Christianity in Modern China,* New Haven & London, Yale University Press, 2010, 197-98.

Although men like Gibson and Burns took the lead in pioneering nineteenth century Protestant missionary work in China, women also played a significant role in this area as well. By 1900, nearly two thirds of missionaries in China were single women, most of them involved in evangelizing, working with women and teaching in schools for girls.[36] As women in Britain gained access to tertiary education in medicine, and qualified, they began to filter through to all the mission fields including China. Agnes Marshall Cowan, for example, one of Edinburgh University's early female graduates in medicine, came to practice in China in 1907. – Apart from a short break in Britain during the First World War, she was to remain in China until shortly before her death in 1940.[37]

Dr. Cowan was one of a remarkable group of Scottish women doctors who brought western medicine to northern Manchuria in the early twentieth century. Despite the problems posed by war, invasion, plague and local hostility, and working often with poor equipment and shortages of drugs, they pioneered a range of medical services, particularly for women, and took a vital role in the development both of the Women's Hospital and the Medical School in Shenyang in Liaoning Province. The outreach in Manchuria of the United Presbyterian Church of Scotland, for whom Dr. Cowan worked, provided a particularly Scottish dimension to missionary engagement in China.

Many claims have been made about the influence female missionaries, and medical missionaries, had on Chinese women – most of which have been overstated. Given the size of China's population, and the small number of missionaries, it is unlikely that most Chinese would have encountered a missionary whether male or female. Female missionaries may have pioneered girls' education in China, and thereby contributed to enhancing women's rights, but it was nationalism, particularly after 1949, that promoted widespread support for the restructuring of

---

36 Welch, I., *Women's Work for Women; Women Missionaries in 19th Century China,* A paper presented to the Eighth Women in Asia Conference, University of Technology, Sydney, 2005.

37 Tsai, H. H., *Scottish Women Medical Pioneers; Manchuria, 1894-1912,* Glasgow, Scottish Medical Journal, the Royal College of Physicians and Surgeons of Glasgow, 1992, 56-59.

Chinese society including a transformation in the role of women.[38] That said, it would be churlish not to acknowledge the stupendous effort, and achievement of women like Dr. Cowan, and her colleagues, in providing western medical care and education in a harsh and difficult environment.

The rigours and routines of missionary life are perhaps best exemplified in the lives of James D. Liddell, his wife Mary, and their family. Throughout their time in China, they lived in trying conditions and were separated from their children who were educated in Britain. The Liddell's were one of many missionary families who, for two generations, worked in China.

A former draper, James Liddell came from the little village of Drymen near Glasgow and studied at the Scottish Congregational College in that city before being appointed as a missionary in China with the LMS in 1898. All four of their children were born in China, the two elder boys, Robert and Eric, being educated at Eltham College for the sons of missionaries and Edinburgh University. Robert later worked as a medical missionary in China. His sister Jenny married Dr. Charles W. Somerville of Dalkeith Congregational Church who served in Wuhan, the capital of Hubei Province.[39]

After winning the four hundred metres at the 1924 Olympics in Paris, Eric worked as a missionary teacher and later as an ordained minister at the Anglo-Chinese College at Tianjin. In 1934 he married Florence the daughter of Hugh and Agnes Mackenzie who ran a boarding house for missionaries in Tianjin under the auspices of the United Church of Canada.[40] Eric and Florence had three children though Eric never saw his third Canadian-born daughter as he died at the Japanese Internment Camp at Weihsien in February 1945.[41] The civilians who emerged from

---

38 Davin, D., *British Women Missionaries in Nineteenth Century China*, London, Taylor & Francis, 1992, 257-271.

39 Calder, J. M., *Scotland's March Past*, London, London Missionary Society, 1945, 25.

40 Grypma, S., *Healing Henan; Canadian Nurses at the North China Mission, 1888-1947*, Vancouver, University of British Columbia Press, 2008, 100.

41 McCasland, D., *Eric Liddell – Pure Gold*, Grand Rapids, Discovery House Publishers, 2001, 281. The Weihsien internment camp was located in the present day

the internment in 1945 camp probably owed their survival to the local Chinese farmers who risked their lives bringing them food and handling messages to family and friends in Europe and North America. Their bravery and generosity of spirit may have been grudgingly admired but was infrequently reciprocated.

Writing in 1817, Robert Morrison famously noted that "the Chinese are generally selfish, cold-blooded and inhumane". Were his views shared by his contemporaries and successors or did less pejorative appraisals emerge as Protestant missionaries engaged in more depth with Chinese people? The dominant thinking in Protestant missionary circles saw Chinese people as in a mindless stupor, morally bankrupt and practising idolatrous rituals. Almost a century later at the Great Missionary Exhibition in London in 1909 these themes continued to resonate. Chinese people were depicted as heathens, absorbed in the world of their bodily senses and "in their blindness" bowing in garish temples before menacing idols.[42] "Buddhist, Taoist or Confucian", explained the historian of the LMS in 1923, "it amounts to the same thing, and the only and universal ritual is the worship of one's ancestors.[43]

But there were more sympathetic and perceptive views amongst the missionary community. "There is a general widespread impression that the Chinese are in all things the opposite of other men", the Edinburgh medical missionary Dugald Christie wrote, "that they never feel or act as other peoples would. Externally there is some truth in this … but when we come to the elemental passions at the foundation of our common human nature … we can grip their hands as brothers for we find them strong, virile, and reliable in those deeper feelings which are the mainspring of action." He decisively rejected the notion that the Chinese were somehow "different". "Their family affection, their staunch friendship, their unselfishness to those they love, their homely joys, their love of children, their kindliness to friends and neighbours,

---

city of Weifang in Shandong Province.

42 Reinders, E., *Borrowed Gods and Foreign Bodies*, Berkley, Los Angeles and London, University of California Press, 2004, 7.

43 James, A. T. S., *Twenty–Five Years of the L.M.S.*, London, London Missionary Society, 1923, 47.

their warm-hearted gratitude, their fortitude in trouble, their patience in enduring, will compare with those of any nation."[44]

Christie's insights into Chinese society were derived from his study and understanding of Chinese culture and religious beliefs. He was familiar with the main themes of Buddhist, Confucian and Taoist thought as well as the dynamics of a society in which the patriarchal family system played an important role. He had a good understanding of traditional Chinese medicine, elements of which he sought to complement western medical practice where appropriate. His empathy with the traditional Chinese virtues of fortitude, hospitality and gratitude, and his skill as a medical practitioner, won him many friends, and contacts, including local magistrates and officials as well as senior military personnel. They were to be valuable allies.

Christie was not slow to enlist the financial and political support of his Chinese friends in Manchuria, first for his fledgling hospital and then for the Medical College at Shenyang which opened with fifty students in 1912. Whilst most of the teaching staff were from abroad, Christie was determined that the College should not be considered as "foreign" and that it would progressively come under the management of Chinese personnel as indeed it did thirty years later. Significantly, Christie pioneered the introduction of the Chinese language in teaching though summaries in English had to be produced of the latest medical research. His high hopes for the College and his students were not unfounded. In 1935 the University of Edinburgh recognised the Shenyang course as qualifying for admission to post graduate medical research at Edinburgh. Christie's unshakable belief that "the Chinese are specially adapted to make good physicians and surgeons" had been vindicated.[45]

Christie's views on the development of medical practice and education in China were set out in a paper he presented to the China Centenary Missionary Conference in Shanghai in 1907.[46] Whilst he envisaged the provision of medical facilities and services evolving within a Christian

---

44 Christie, D., *Thirty Years in Moukden, 1883-1913*, London, Constable and Company, 1914, 60.

45 Christie, *op. cit.,* 276.

46 Centenary Conference Committee, *Records; China Centenary Missionary Conference*, Shanghai, Methodist Publishing House, 1907, 247 – 68.

missionary framework, his vision of China-wide medical care was both bold and comprehensive. Although recognising that funding and providing sufficient personnel might be problematic, Christie demanded nothing less than a medical centre in every large town. Outreach from these centres would extend to rural areas through the establishment of dispensaries and regular visits by nursing and medical staff. In particular, he identified the need for drug addicts, lepers and the mentally ill to be provided with additional services to facilitate their treatment. All these measures would be complemented by a comprehensive public health education programme aimed at the future good health of the nation.

Christie's long years in Shenyang and unremitting toil began to take their toll and in 1923 he retired to Edinburgh in poor health. Apart from a brief return visit in 1925, the remainder of his life was devoted to finding support for the Medical College he had founded and trying to interpret Chinese life and society to enquiring Scottish minds. He maintained close contacts with Chinese visitors and students in Scotland and in 1929 helped found, and was appointed Honorary President of, the Sino-Scottish Society in Edinburgh.[47] Internationally recognised and honoured, he was particularly gratified to be appointed a Fellow of the Royal Scottish Geographical Society in 1930 in recognition of his work and travels in Manchuria.

Christie's vision of China's future was to be clouded first by the Japanese invasion and then shattered by the war and revolution that followed. And the China which emerged was to be very different from that which he had known. Nevertheless, his extraordinary contribution to Chinese medicine and society were not to be completely eradicated as his Medical College was to form the nucleus of what is now the renowned China Medical University in Shenyang.[48]

By contrast, how did Chinese people regard the missionaries who were perhaps closer to them than most other foreigners? Whilst missionaries were certainly seen as instruments of change, and promoters of

---

47 *The Scotsman*, 18 February 1930.

48 Scottish Churches China Group, *A Picture History 1883-2003; From Mukden Medical College to No. 2 Clinical College of China Medical University*, Edinburgh, Scottish Churches China Group, 2004.

modernity, they were also perceived by many Chinese as subverting traditional culture and values. Moreover, whilst missionaries sought to integrate into and identify with Chinese society, they were frequently ambivalent and unsure how to respond when domestic political events and violence affected them personally. In the main, many were insensitive to the needs and aspirations of Chinese Christians, dominating the nascent Chinese church and introducing largely irrelevant denominational considerations. Later to lead the Chinese Home Missionary Society, Glasgow educated Cheng Jingyi told a rather startled Edinburgh audience in 1910 that "your denominationalism does not interest Chinese Christians" and that the Chinese "had never understood it, could not delight in it though they often suffered from it".[49] His proposals for an independent ecumenical Chinese church were acknowledged but missionary support for such an undertaking was far from unanimous.

Although missionaries were seen by their supporters in Scotland as being at the forefront of Christian endeavour, the idealised, often mystical, portrayal of missionary life was mostly at variance with reality. "Above is heaven, below is Hangzhou" goes the Chinese saying referring to the city that Marco Polo described as one of the most beautiful in the world. Duncan Main remembered differently –

"the constant contact with heathenism, the assault on one's special senses, living among people that are immoral, dirty superstitious, untruthful and lovers of pleasure more than lovers of God; and these influences have to be felt to be understood; the depression caused by the climate, the great heat, the constant dampness which is sometimes overwhelming; the effect of fleas, mosquitoes, centipedes and many other insect pests, not to mention snakes, rats and other vermin, make inroads on one's nerves; the difficulties of travel, of food going wrong in the heat, bad drinking water, wells poisoned with surface sewage, people misunderstanding your good intentions, trying to get as much out of you as they can, and making you pay exorbitant prices ... The great difficulties of speaking the language, and the trial of not being able to speak and preach as well as you would

---

49 Lian Xi, *op. cit.,* 35. Cheng was educated at the Anglo-Chinese College in Beijing, the LMS Theological School in Tianjin and the Bible Training Institute in Glasgow (1906-08).

*like. Cut off from home, friends, fellowship and the stimulating influ-
ences of intellectual and religious life in the "dear homeland", not
sufficient to pray and love."*[50]

Probably very few in Scotland realised just how difficult missionary life
could be in China, or, indeed, elsewhere overseas.

Given the circumstances in which they lived, missionaries looked forward with anticipation to returning on leave but often found themselves
increasingly unfamiliar with the "dear homeland" after years of living
abroad.

Apart from seeing family, children and friends, however, there was
much to be done. Missionary support organisations like Edinburgh
University's Student Volunteer Missionary Union had to be addressed,
sermons delivered, funds raised and new staff interviewed. Missionary
life and activities were frequently popularised by lantern slides and, later, cine film. These evening presentations must have added a dash of co-
lour, if not romance, to a dull winter evening whether in the countryside
or in town. Whoever spoke, they were normally introduced as being
associated with a distant, heathen, interesting, if somewhat frighten-
ing, location. Dugald Christie was known as Christie of Mukden whilst
Duncan Main was introduced by the name he was known by in China
- Dr Apricot of Heaven-below.

Reflecting the religious interests and spiritual priorities of their times,
Scottish missionaries worked as pastors, preachers and teachers, often
in remote, inhospitable locations where their faith, and vocation, were
sorely tested. Protestant missionaries in general, and Scottish Christians
in particular, probably lend themselves to a high degree of stereotyping
which tends to diminish their achievements and, indeed, their human-
ity. Of course, like many expatriates, there were some who never really engaged with China or the Chinese but they seem to have been a
small minority. However, despite the difficulties they faced, living in
a rapidly changing society, which was itself redefining its future, the
views of men like Christie and Main on Chinese society were, almost

---

50 De Gruche, *op. cit.*, 95.

always, fresh, challenging, never complacent and driven by a strong commitment to China's people.

What legacy did these Scottish Protestants leave to China? Many of their activities had considerable merit. They did nurture an indigenous church in the European reformed tradition even if its future structure and development would have surprised them. They did help people by establishing medical and educational facilities. They did act as agents of change, opening up vistas of a wider world beyond both China and Scotland. But, at the same time, many of their claims about themselves and China were simply wrong. Despite their best efforts to integrate, they always remained foreigners, haunted by association with Britain's promotion of the opium trade and aggressive commercial expansion. Although many thought they understood Chinese society, most saw it as flawed and inferior. And their pious hope that China would be readily converted to a northern European derived version of Christianity was never realistic then – and never will be.

4 Tea and More from China

*There are few sights more pleasing than a Chinese family
in the interior engaged in gathering the tea leaves.*

ROBERT FORTUNE.

The import into Britain of tea from China increased dramatically
during the nineteenth century. Some eleven million kilos of tea
arrived in 1819, twenty nine million kilos in 1853 and over fifty
seven million kilos ten years later, making Britain the highest per head
tea consumer in the world. Tea had become Britain's national drink.

As elsewhere in Britain, tea permeated many aspects of Scottish culture.
Tea tables and tea caddies became a part of everyday domestic life. Tea
dances were held in fashionable homes across the country. Factory owners encouraged their workers to drink tea, rather than alcohol, as it was
less likely to lead to industrial accidents. Kate Cranston capitalised on
the social acceptability of tea, opening her first Tea Room in Glasgow's
Ingram Street in 1886. The 1888 International Exhibition in Glasgow
boasted the Bishop's Palace Tea Rooms, run by J. Lyons & Co., with
waitresses dressed in Mary Stuart costumes.[51]

Because importing tea was highly profitable, many companies employed
their own buyers in Guangzhou. William Melrose from Edinburgh first
lived there from 1842 to 1847 when he learnt the ins and outs of the

---

51 Forrest, D., *Tea for the British*, London, Chatto & Windus, 1973, 183.

trade as a tea taster. He returned to Guangzhou in August 1848, but this time as a buyer for his father's business, William Melrose & Company of Edinburgh.

Life was not easy in Guangzhou. Foreigners lived in cramped, unhealthy conditions outside the city by the river. A friend of William's father had suggested once that, whilst China might be the residence of the Son of Heaven, "it is very far from being heaven, although it may be perhaps a short cut to it." Lawlessness was a real concern and often near at hand. Four of William's friends were attacked by pirates with fire pots near the Bogue Forts after a shooting expedition downriver from Guangzhou. Only after eight pirates had been killed did the remainder flee "swearing they would soon be back again"[52]

Melrose's letters to his father and business associates provide us with a revealing insight into what life was like for a serious minded young man doing business in China in these years. He had many of the attributes for which his countrymen were both renowned and derided. He worked extremely hard and was meticulous in ensuring that his terms of trade and pricing were as sharp as possible. He kept a close eye on his competitors. Planning to ship tea direct to Scotland, he decided not to approach Jardine Matheson for a vessel "because they would directly conclude where she was going to be sent and most likely fill her themselves and send her before I could secure another vessel. The necessity of keeping the matter secret makes it much more troublesome to get a proper vessel."[53]

In addition to the problems of securing ships at reasonable cost, there were the vagaries of the mails which often led to misunderstandings or the countermanding of instructions already executed. Responses to inbound mail were normally composed quickly before the vessel left port again. And sometimes mail simply disappeared – though the Hong Kong postmaster assured William that his name was "familiar to everyone in his office and that was unlikely to happen."[54]

---

52 Mui, H, C. and Mui, L.H., (Eds.) *William Melrose in China 1845-1855*, Edinburgh, Scottish History Society, 1973, 221.

53 Mui and Mui, *op. cit.,* 57.

54 Mui and Mui, *op. cit.,* 165.

The weather in Guangzhou could be trying as well – hot and humid in summer but nearly freezing in winter when his fingers were numb and it was hard to write. That notwithstanding, he took a cold shower every morning which he felt made him glow and lifted his spirits. But there were comforts as well. In April 1850 he wrote to ask if Baird, the wine merchant of Princes Street in Edinburgh, could send him eighty dozen bottles of beer – with characteristic thoroughness he estimated he would use three bottles of beer per day for himself and friends.[55]

Although Melrose was preoccupied with his tea business, he traded in other goods as well. Home to Scotland went a pair of very large jars, silk screens framed in ebony and inlaid with mother of pearl, model boats, camphor wood chests, men and women's clothing, lacquered ware and lanterns. However, whilst the Guangzhou trade was still relatively secure, and he was making a good living, he sensed, correctly, that Shanghai would emerge as the major trading centre in the country.

Traditionally, tea was shipped from Guangzhou but it was invariably inferior in quality to teas available elsewhere in China. With the opening of the Yangzi valley to trade after 1860, tea became available for export from Hankou nearly a thousand kilometres upriver from Shanghai. Now part of the modern day city of Wuhan, the capital of Hubei Province, Hankou is located at the confluence of the Han and Yangzi rivers and was an important trading centre.

Depending on how it was dried, tea was either black or green. Nearly all the tea imported to Britain from China was black with the green tea going mostly to North America. Of the crops cultivated on small holdings across much of China, the first picking of the season was noted for its flavour and fragrance - and value. As demand increased for what became known as new season, or "first chop", tea more and more was exported. It soon became apparent that financial success turned on getting the first pick of the new crop back to Britain as quickly as possible. However, the largest sailing vessels of their day, the East Indiamen, could take six months, and more, to make that journey. What was required were vessels able to complete the journey in half the time taken by the "tea wagons" as they were called.

---

55 Mui and Mui, *op. cit.*, 94 and 234.

Scottish shipbuilders came to play a significant role in the construction of sailing ships that were to replace the East Indiamen. Developed specifically to service the China tea trade, they became known as tea clippers – sleek, square rigged and triple masted, they literally "clipped" through the waves. They were, perhaps, the most elegant, and certainly the fastest, commercial sailing vessels ever built with an average speed of sixteen knots.

Alexander Hall & Sons of Aberdeen led the way in constructing vessels with the forward curving "Aberdeen" bow which gave the foresails a large spread and enhanced speed. Launched in 1839 for the Aberdeen to London route, the twin masted, top-sail schooner, *The Scottish Maid*, was the prototype for many clippers built in Scotland. Other clippers quickly followed notably *Sea Witch*, and the very fast *Reindeer*, both launched in 1848.

As the reputation of Aberdeen ships became widely known, more orders were placed. Built specifically to transport Jardine Matheson's teas from China, *Stornoway*, launched at the end of 1850, was larger than any other vessel built at Hall's yard – and very fast.[56] Not without pride, the *Aberdeen Journal* noted a year later that "*Stornoway*, another clipper recently launched here, made the run home from Whampoa to London in 103 days, coming down the China Sea against the full strength of the south-west monsoon, and accomplishing the distance between the Cape of Good Hope and London in 37 days. So far as this season's rivalry between British and American clippers in the China trade has been tested by their performances, the British builders have the best of it".[57]

Jardine Matheson was clearly pleased and another clipper from Hall's yard, *Cairngorm*, joined their fleet in 1853. Later that year, she set the record of a hundred and ten days for the passage between London and Hong Kong. Launched in 1851 for Taylor and Potter of Liverpool, *Chrysolite* also had a formidable reputation for speed, winning the race to bring the new season's tea to Britain in 1852 with a journey time of a hundred and five days from Whampoa to Liverpool.

---

56 MacGregor, D. R., *The Tea Clippers,* London, Percival, Marshall & Co. Ltd., 1952, 48.

57 *Aberdeen Journal*, Aberdeen, 10 December 1851.

The tea race from China to Britain started that year with clippers vying with one another to land the first crop of new season tea. The route chosen for the voyage home was dependent on the prevailing winds, but most Masters set a course directly down the China Sea, through the Formosa Channel, and then north of the Paracels. From there they courted the land and sea breezes down the coast of south Vietnam (Cochinchina), and then Borneo, before heading for the Indian Ocean through the Sunda Straight between Sumatra and Java. Alternative routes were to sail down the west side of the Philippines, through the Sulu Sea and Celebes Sea, to the Lombok Straight between Bali and Lombok, or to sail from the China coast down the east side of the Philippines, and then, via the Spice Islands, to the Ombai Straight north of Timor. Once in the Indian Ocean, clippers sailed west to round the Cape of Good Hope, then west of the Canary Islands and on to the south coast of England.

Interest in the outcome of these annual races was intense both in Britain and China. The Captain and crew knew they would be collecting a sizeable bounty if their vessel was first to land the new season's tea. There was great excitement when the inbound vessels were identified in the English Channel and their progress was carefully monitored. Bets were placed on which vessel would be first to land the new season's tea on the wharf. In one tense tea broker's saleroom, there was even a wind indicator, operated from a vane on the roof, to help monitor the speed of the clipper carrying his tea![58]

Just as there was competition to bring the new season's tea from China, there was also competition in the design and construction of clippers. Trained as a shipwright, Walter Hood opened his yard in Aberdeen adjacent to his rivals, Alexander Hall & Sons, in 1839. Most of his vessels were built for the Aberdeen White Star Line for use as merchantmen and in the emigration trade to Australia. Many had a reputation for speed – *Phoenician*, for example, completing the Sydney to London passage in eighty three days in 1851-52 under the formidable Captain Sproat. However, Hood is probably best remembered for *Thermopylae*, the graceful clipper that raced *Cutty Sark* from Shanghai to London in 1872 – and won. The journey took just a hundred and fifteen days.

---

58 MacGregor, *op. cit.*, 13.

Built specifically for the tea trade to compete with *Thermopylae*, it was not by chance that *Cutty Sark* was constructed on the Clyde which was to overtake Aberdeen, and other ports, as the leading centre for clipper construction in Britain. The river was home to a large number of innovative naval architects and engineers.[59] *Cutty Sark* was designed by the marine surveyor, Hercules Linton from Inverbervie, who had trained with Alexander Hall & Sons in Aberdeen. With the engineer, William Dundas Scott, he formed Scott & Linton, Shipbuilders, their yard being on the River Leven near where it joins the Clyde at Dumbarton. It is not clear why the new company was awarded the contract for *Cutty Sark* as it had never built such a large vessel and, eventually, it went into liquidation. The vessel was completed by William Denny & Sons, and launched in November 1869.

Built of wood, or iron, or both, the shipyards down the river as far as Greenock produced ships of different compositions and designs but all recognisable as tea clippers; all were built for speed. In 1863 the Greenock firm, Robert Steele & Co., launched the first composite clipper used in the China trade, *Taeping,* having earlier been successful with the wooden hulled *Young Lochinvar* and *Sercia*. The renowned Charles Connell of the newly established Scotstoun Shipyard also built vessels for the China trade, including *Taitsing, Spindrift* and *Windhover*.

Alexander Stephen & Sons launched clippers, notably *Eliza Shaw* in 1863 and *Forward Ho* in 1867. *Lord of the Isles,* built by Robert Scott & Co. of Greenock, was the first iron-hulled tea clipper. Launched in 1853, she is remembered for losing the 1856 tea race by only ten minutes to the American clipper, *Maury* and for her remarkable ninety day passage from Shanghai to London in 1858.[60]

Clyde-built clippers were noted not only for their perfect proportion and balance but also for their yacht-like finish. All their woodwork on deck or below was of the finest teak or mahogany "so beautifully fashioned as to bear comparison with the work of a first-class cabinet-maker, whilst bulwark rails, stanchions, skylights, capstans and binnacles shone with

---

59 The John Elder Chair of Naval Architecture and Ocean Engineering was endowed by Isabella Elder in memory of her late husband, the shipbuilder John Elder, in 1883.

60 The repeal of the Navigation Acts in 1849 in line with *laissez faire* thinking allowed American ships to compete freely with their British counterparts.

more brass-work than is ever found in a modern yacht."[61] The fine work-manship demanded of those building tea clippers on the Clyde certainly contributed to the river's supremacy in ship construction.

There was often a very clear Scottish involvement in the commissioning and operation of clippers. *Lord of the Isles* was built for Maxton & Co. of Greenock in 1853. Launched in 1865, *Taitsing* was built for Longmuir & Findlay also of Greenock.[62] Captain Alexander Roger of Cellardyke owned the *Taeping* which, ninety nine days out of Fuzhou, famously beat *Ariel* by twenty minutes in the 1866 tea race. Of the eighty five British registered tea clippers launched between 1850 and 1870, forty nine were built in Scotland, two thirds of them on the Clyde.[63]

Crack Scottish Masters commanded some of the best clippers. John Robertson from Lewis was Master, consecutively, of *Cairngorm*, *John o' Gaunt* and *Stornoway*; John Ryrie, also from Lewis, is remembered for his time in command of *Cairngorm* and *Flying Spur;* John MacKinnon from Tiree was Master of *Taeping* whilst his great rival, John Keay from Anstruther, commanded *Ariel*. Scottish nautical connections with China at this time were not restricted to clippers and their crews. Perhaps one of the best known Shanghai pilots then was Hughie Sutherland who hailed from Caithness. He was remembered for his navigational skills – when he was sober.[64] There were obviously hazards, other than pirates, on the China coast!

Over the years, there were direct imports of tea by clippers to both the Clyde and Forth but these tailed off largely as a result of the efficiency of the coastal trade between the Thames and Scotland and the use of fast rail freight links between London and Scotland. Whilst clippers carried mainly tightly packed boxes of tea on their demanding passages from China, slower sailing vessels, and later steamships, carried other mer-chandise to the west including silk, porcelain and knick-knacks. The volume of imports coming directly to Scotland was very small but por-celain and silk would have certainly found their way north from London, or via the Swedish East India Company in Gothenburg or the Dutch

---

61 Lubbock, B., *The China Clippers*, Glasgow, James Brown & Son, 1914, 144.

62 MacGregor, *op. cit.,* 163.

63 Lubbock, *op. cit.,* Appendix A.

64 Lubbock, *op. cit.,* 177.

East India Company in Rotterdam, both of which had strong links with Scotland.

It is ironic that the year which saw the launching of *Cutty Sark* also marked the opening of the Suez Canal in 1869. Steamships using the new waterway could make the journey to China in half the time a clipper might take to sail by the Cape of Good Hope. Steamships cut the round trip journey time from some two hundred days to around one hundred and twenty. Moreover, individual vessels could make two or three roundtrips a year thereby ensuring that, not only new season tea, but other teas as well, were readily available throughout the year. The era of the elegant tea clippers was over.

The Clyde was well placed to exploit the steamship market both for China and elsewhere. Already with a sound reputation for marine design, shipbuilding and engineering, a developed industrial hinterland and ready local availability of coal and ironstone, the Clyde took the lead in the construction, first, of ironclad vessels and, then, larger vessels built of steel powered by compound engines. As shipbuilding replaced trade as the major activity on the river, the Clyde was acknowledged as the premier shipbuilding centre of the Empire with Clyde-built vessels setting the international benchmark for quality and reliability.

Individual shipyards on the river formed close relationships with their customers. The British Steam Navigation Company bought mostly from Barclay Curle & Co.; orders from the Peninsular and Oriental Steam Navigation Company went, in the main, to Cairds of Greenock; the China Navigation Company favoured Scott's of Greenock with much of its business. By the time Scott & Co. ceased trading in 1993, the company had built over one thousand two hundred and fifty vessels at Greenock, of which ninety five were for the China Navigation Company/John Swire & Sons. Denny's of Dumbarton built the *Pioneer* which was assembled in Shanghai. It was the first commercial vessel to sail unaided through the Yangzi gorges to Chongqing (Chunking) in 1900 under Captain Samuel Plant who surveyed much of the river.

Clyde expertise was not limited to shipbuilding alone. To meet the needs of shipping companies operating in China and the region, like the China Navigation Company, and the Blue Funnel line, it soon became apparent that a local ship repair facility would be a desirable and profitable investment.

James Henry Scott, by then Senior Partner of John Swire & Sons, oversaw the development of the Taikoo Dockyard at Quarry Bay on the north shore of Hong Kong Island between 1902 and 1907. Skilled Scottish engineers and tradesmen were involved in the construction of the dockyard itself. Many later found employment there and at the rival Hong Kong and Whampoa Dock Company in Kowloon. "Where eastern seas bubble up hot to the flame of an equatorial sun", Gordon Casserly wrote in 1905, "Chinese workmen with Scotch overseers turn out 6,000 ton steel ships and do battleship repairing worthy of Woolwich or Devonport."[65] These emigrant Scots are remembered today in streets in the area like Braemar Terrace and Braemar Hill behind it.

As they sipped tea on their verandas overlooking Hong Kong's harbour, some of these emigrant Scots might have wondered why some tea came from India rather than China. From the beginning of the nineteenth century, the burgeoning demand for tea began to focus entrepreneurial minds on the possibility of cultivating tea other than in China. Following the Treaty of Nanjing in 1842, many British investors were concerned that the Chinese might legalise the cultivation of home grown opium thereby wrecking the financial arrangements underpinning the lucrative tea trade. William Bentinck, Governor–General of Bengal, established a Committee in 1834 to explore the feasibility of growing tea in India. The Committee's secretary, a young Scot called George James Gordon, was despatched in 1834 and 1836 to Macau to obtain plants and workers. He came back with various batches of seed which were raised in the nursery plantations of Assam and in south India.[66] However, tea from Chinese seeds and plants was also to be grown in the Himalayas, largely through the efforts of an able, brave and tenacious Scotsman, Robert Fortune, who was born in 1812 at the small hamlet of Kelloe in the Scottish borders.

---

65 Casserly, G., *The Land of the Boxers; Or China Under the Allies*, London, Longmans & Green, 1903, 54.
66 Le Pichon, A., *China Trade and Empire,* Oxford, Oxford University Press for the British Academy, 2006, 245.

Like many young men from a poor rural background, Fortune trained locally as a gardener before making his way to Edinburgh in search of work. He was fortunate in obtaining employment in Edinburgh's Royal Botanic Garden then under the dynamic curatorship of William McNab. Originally founded in 1670 as Scotland's first physic garden for medicinal plants, the Garden was entering an exciting phase when Fortune joined the staff in 1840. The Garden had just been moved to its current location in the grounds of Inverleith House where there was plenty of space for new planting. Under the stimulus of Enlightenment thinking, and the travels of men like Captain Cook, botany was emerging as a new discipline which went far beyond the immediate interests of physicians and surgeons. With the wealth generated from the Caribbean, through sugar and the slave trade, and from India as a result of political patronage, wealthy Scots – the nabobs – were returning home to build fine houses with gardens. There was a growing demand for exotic and interesting plants, not just from this new, wealthy elite, but from traditional landowners as well. Fortune was determined to be part of this exciting development. With the support of McNab, he secured the post of Superintendent of the Royal Horticultural Society's Hothouse Department at Chiswick Garden in London. Less than a year later, he was appointed the Society's Collector in China, arriving in Hong Kong in June 1843. It marked the beginning of a momentous eighteen year association with China which saw him travelling to places where few, if any, Europeans had ever ventured.

Fortune lived up to his name though his task was not easy as he was regarded initially with fear and suspicion by most of the Chinese people he encountered. To overcome this, he had his head shaved, donned a wig with a queue and wore Chinese dress. More importantly, he started to learn Chinese which gave him an insight into the attitudes, and thinking, of ordinary people whom he met on his travels. "I have been constantly among them," he wrote "wandering over and among their hills, dining in their houses and sleeping in their temples." Whilst there were doubtless some "bad characters", those living in the remoter inland parts of the country he found to be "quiet, civil and obliging."[67]

---

67 Fortune, R., *Three Years Wanderings in the Northern Provinces of China*, London, John Murray, 2nd. Edition, 1847, xv and xvi.

Looking for plants in the hinterland of the treaty ports was challenging. He was frequently chased away from villages, assaulted or even, on one occasion, attacked by pirates. But he persevered, shipping back to London a variety of plants new to the western world. These included oil rape seed (*Brassica chinensis*), the Japanese snowball tree (*Viburnum 'plicatum v. Sterile*), the kumquat (*Fortunella*), winter jasmine (*Jasminum nudiflorum*) and a host of azeleas. The variety was endless such that, as Ann Lindsay has noted, "all year long a Fortune plant is flowering in Britain"[68]

His quest to "discover" new plants led him in 1844 to Suzhou (Soochow) located on the Grand Canal by the lower reaches of the Yangzi River in Jiangsu Province. As he looked at the pretty houses, with their large lanterns, the street stalls, the elegant women and the happy throng of people milling around the bridges over the Canal, he couldn't help but feel a sense of "secret triumph" at being, probably, the first westerner to visit the "most fashionable city of the Celestial Empire."[69] His disguise had stood him well. And he would use it again later.

Fortune kept a diary and notes of his travels which were published by John Murray in 1847 shortly after he returned to London. His *Three Years Wandering in the Northern Provinces of China* was an immediate success. It was read by another remarkable Scot, the botanist John Forbes Royale, formerly Professor of Materia Medica at King's College, London who came to visit Fortune at Chiswick in May 1848 with a proposal on behalf of the EIC. It was one which Fortune could not refuse.

Born in Kanpur, Royale had served as an assistant surgeon with the EIC, eventually becoming superintendent of the company's gardens at Saharanpur in Uttar Pradesh in northern India. Given his wide botanical experience, Royale was convinced that tea could be grown in India if the right plants could be obtained. His proposal on behalf of the EIC was that Fortune return to China, obtain good quality stock and ship it to India together with tea makers, and their equipment, to ensure this new venture got off to a flying start. Both Fortune and Royale knew the dangers involved as the Chinese had jealously guarded the secret of growing and producing tea. Recognising that he was undertaking what

---

68 Lindsay, A., *Seeds of Blood and Beauty*, Edinburgh, Birlinn, 2005, 269.
69 Lindsay, *op. cit.*, 260-61.

today might be called industrial espionage, Fortune's remuneration was to be generous.[70]

Just over five years after he first visited China, Fortune arrived back in the autumn of 1848. During his earlier visit he had learnt that green tea and black tea came from the same plant – until then it was supposed they came from different plants.[71] More importantly, however, he knew where he should be looking for healthy seed and plants to send abroad. The stock he collected would be shipped in newly invented, sealed, glass and wood cases which provided some protection against the elements on the long sea journey from China to India.[72]

Between 1848 and 1851 Fortune made two major expeditions into the interior of China. In 1848, accompanied by two servants, Wang and a coolie known only as such, he headed first by way of the Yangzi valley to the mountainous tea producing districts of Zhejiang and Anhui Provinces. His goal was Sung Lo mountain (Songluoshan) renowned for the high quality green tea grown on its slopes.

His journey by riverboat, sedan chair and on foot was not uneventful but its outcome far exceeded his expectations. He stayed comfortably in the house of Wang's father and was able to obtain a good collection of tea seeds and young plants. During his visit, he gained a rare insight into the life of a Chinese peasant family who treated him with much kindness – even if he was a curiosity. Drawing on his rural background, and engaging with his hosts, Fortune mused that the "cottages amongst the tea hills are simple and rude in their construction, and remind one of what we used to see in Scotland in former years, when the cow and pig lived and fed in the same house with the peasant."[73] Perhaps agrarian change came to Scotland long before it came to China but, at the time when he was writing, there were still many cottages in rural Scotland where the cow and the pig shared the same living space as their owners!

---

70 Rose, S., *For All the Tea in China*, London, Random House, 2009, 6.

71 Fortune discovered that green tea is not fermented whereas black tea is.

72 Known as Wardian cases, they were invented by Dr. Nathaniel Bagshaw Ward of London around 1829. They greatly facilitated the transfer of plants around the world.

73 Fortune, *op. cit.*, 193.

Returning to Shanghai, Fortune prepared his seeds and plants for shipment to Kolkata, accompanying them as far as Hong Kong. Later, on a dull and wet evening in May 1849 he set out from Ningbo on his second expedition, this time to the Wuyi mountains (Wuyishan) in the north west of Fujian Province where some of the best black tea in China was grown. "I felt rather low-spirited," he wrote later, "I could not conceal from my mind that the journey ... was a long one, and perhaps full of dangers."[74]

And adventures he had! The riverboat he was travelling on was seized because of unpaid debts and its sail taken away; he was thronged by beggars; only his dexterity eating with chopsticks saved him from being recognised as a foreigner; he teetered along perilous mountain paths - but, eventually after many days climbing, one of the grandest sights he had ever beheld was there before him, the Wuyi mountains. "Never in my life had I seen such a view as this, so grand, so sublime. High ranges of mountains were towering on my right and on my left ... as far as the eye could reach, the whole country seemed broken up into mountains and hills of all heights, with peaks of every form"[75] This was the best tea growing country in China.

He found accommodation in a Buddhist monastery where his companions were gracious and gentle. Often accompanied by a monk, he hastened to collect the black tea plants he had journeyed so far to find. In the autumn of 1849, he returned with them to Shanghai from where they were shipped to India.

The last piece of the jigsaw was the workers who would tend the fragile plants now in India and harvest the first crop. Through his contacts in Shanghai, Fortune recruited a group of experienced young men who, together with their equipment, he accompanied to northern India in 1851. Although some of the seeds and plants he had sent from China did not survive, the majority did. Under the care of a young Scots Surgeon-Major of the Indian Medical Service, Archibald Campbell, the new plants flourished in the mountainous Darjeeling region of West Bengal.

---

74 Fortune, R., *A Journey to the Tea Countries of China*, London, John Murray, 1852, 160.

75 Fortune, *op. cit.*, *Journey*, 211.

Robert Fortune didn't initiate the growing of tea in India, but he certainly redefined and reinvigorated it. Within a generation British consumption of tea from India and Ceylon accounted for over eighty five per cent of tea imports; consumption of tea from China nosedived to less than ten per cent from sixty two million kilos in 1879 to some ten million kilos twenty five years later. Reasons are not hard to discern. Indian and Ceylonese teas were rushed off to market as soon as they were ready. The Chinese continued the time tried system of getting together large quantities of tea, often of different quality, before shipment which often resulted in staleness. Moreover, although competition remained strong, tea from the subcontinent was more often than not cheaper than tea from China.[76]

Robert Fortune saw his role as promoting the development, and transfer, of useful, and beautiful plants, around the British imperial world as an undertaking that would benefit many people. He longed for the day when botanists, plant collectors and travellers would have unrestricted access to the Chinese interior. His vision, in many ways, became reality - but his legacy to China was a bitter one.

---

76 Forrest, *op. cit., Journey*, 162 and 188.

5 Living in Interesting Times

> *May you live in interesting times!*
>
> CHINESE CURSE.

Scots were involved in civil administration and public order interventions in China during the nineteenth and twentieth centuries, largely arising from efforts to open up trade and protect the perceived interests of businessmen, missionaries and others associated with British influence in China. Even with the advent of the nationalist movement, many commentators continued to regard China as a hopeless case, steeped in superstition and corruption and incapable of being rehabilitated along tried and tested western lines. Writing in 1926, the American journalist, Rodney Gilbert, wrote –

> *"What is wrong with China and will continue to be wrong with her, is that the Chinese are children, that their world is a world of child's make believe, and that they have no more right, in their own interest or in humanity's larger interest, to govern themselves or shape their own course of education, than pupils in a school have to boss the faculty and to dictate what they will learn and what they will not."*[77]

His views would have been acceptable to very many, though perhaps not all, expatriates in China, including many of those who joined the Consular Service, and the Maritime Customs Service, in China.

---

77 Gilbert, R., *What's wrong with China*, New York, Frederick A. Stokes, 1926, 45.

The Consular Service emerged following the 1842 Treaty of Nanjing which allowed British residents to live in the newly opened treaty ports where they were subject to the extraterritorial jurisdiction of consuls appointed by the British Foreign Office rather than to Chinese officials and courts. The role of these consuls was subsequently extended to other new treaty ports as they were opened after 1860.

The Service in China comprised a small group of officers, sometimes accompanied by their families, who served in different parts of China where there was a need for British interests to be represented. Consuls were involved in liaising with the Chinese authorities, usually local officials, to ensure compliance with treaty obligations, whilst not infrequently seeking to restrain the ambitions of overbearing British missionaries and traders who often had little sensitivity to Chinese interests and concerns. Consuls also administered civil and criminal justice to resident and visiting British citizens, not infrequently drunken, violent sailors from British registered vessels. Certainly, the China coast was known to be a wet one!

Before the advent of the telegraph, and sometimes even after that, consuls often had to take major decisions which might impact on wider British - Chinese relations without the advice, or support, of senior personnel who were far away in Beijing, Guangzhou or Shanghai. Their work was difficult, demanding and often dangerous but, almost to a man, they gained an unprecedented understanding of a society on the cusp of change.

Only three hundred and nine appointments were made to the Service in the century between 1843 and 1943 when Britain surrendered its extraterritorial rights in China. For most of this period, there was an average of sixty officers in post at any one time. Because of its size, promotion prospects within the Service were poor and pay levels derisory. Despite this, the Service attracted recruits, many of whom had a genuine interest in China and the Chinese even if their subsequent experiences did not live up to their expectations!

Less than ten per cent of those appointed to the Service were Scots. Right from the early days, there were concerns about Chinese being spoken with a broad "Scotch or Irish" accent and calls for the Civil

Service Commission to exclude those with a strong "provincial" accent. When open competition for entry was eventually introduced in 1872, Scots candidates found themselves far removed from the London based crammers which sought to facilitate entry to the Service.

Like the modern Colonial Administrative Service, which was to emerge in 1932, the Consular Service in China had a strong southern English, middle class ethos which accepted that "a better type of man" could probably be found in the English Public Schools, and Oxbridge, rather than from the Scottish universities whose graduates came from a more diversified social background.[78] Although some of the Scots recruited to the Service came from professional, middle class families associated with education, the church and the law, others had more humble origins being the children of builders, labourers or tailors.

One of the earlier Scots Consuls appointed was Robert Thom from Glasgow whose uncle was a trading partner of William Jardine. Thom first went to work in the piece-goods department of Jardine Matheson in Guangzhou in 1833 where he learnt to speak Chinese fluently. He acted as one of the few official linguists during the first Anglo-Chinese War between 1839 and 1842. He was subsequently appointed Consul in Ningbo where he died in 1846.[79] George Macdonald Home Playfair from St Andrews came from a well-known medical colonial family. As well as having a scholarly interest in botany, he published a geographical dictionary, *The Cities and Towns of China*, in 1879. Playfair was adept at cultivating good relations with the Chinese authorities. Whilst Consul in Ningbo in the late 1890s, he invited the provincial commander-in-chief, and other officials with their families, to the consulate's Christmas Eve children's party complete with Christmas tree and lights. Everyone, particularly the children, seemed to have a happy time.[80]

Perhaps more conventional was George Jamieson from Banffshire who, after thirty five years of service, retired as Consul-General at Shanghai in 1899. Based on his experience as a Judge of the Supreme Court

---

78 Coates, P. D., *The China Consuls; British Consular Officers, 1843-1943*, Oxford, Oxford University Press, 1988, 79, 80, 428.

79 Le Pichon, A., *China Trade and Empire*, Oxford, Oxford University Press for the British Academy, 2006, 184.

80 Coates, *op. cit.*, 216-17.

in Shanghai, he published subsequently in 1921 *Chinese Family and Commercial Law* in an attempt to systematise Chinese legal practice for foreigners.[81] Regarded as a safe pair of hands by the Foreign Office, he represented the British and Chinese Corporation in seeking railway and other concessions in China for British industrial and trading interests. His grandson was Hugh Gaitskell, leader of the Opposition in Britain, and leader of the Labour Party, from 1955 to 1963.

Whilst there were honours, and riches, for those who reached the higher ranks, the Service was not without its dangers and demands. Scots were affected like everyone else. D. Oliphant was killed during the Boxer rising whilst J. P. M. Fraser was dismissed for drunkenness. A. S. Harvey was required to resign because of "mental derangement" probably as a result of living in remote Beihai (Pakhoi) - the Foreign Office telegram to his parents said simply "I am ... to acquaint you that ... your son has become insane".[82] Nevertheless, service in China remained an attractive career option with, for example, George Jamieson's son following him into the Consular Service.

When he died in 1925 Alexander Hosie had visited all the Provinces of China except Xinjiang. The son of a poor Scottish farmer from Inverurie, he paid for his university education by tutoring other students. After completing his language studies in China, he was sent on special duties to Chongqing in Sichuan Province in the far west of China. He travelled extensively during his three years there, recording his experiences in *Three Years in Western China*, which was published in 1889. He twice served at the other end of China in Yingkou (Newchwang) in Manchuria where he again travelled extensively, writing about his adventures in *Manchuria; its People, Resources and Recent History* published in 1901. An adventurer, publicist and scholar, Hosie did much to enlighten western opinion about the challenges facing rural Chinese society at a time of change.

Like the China Consular Service, the Imperial Maritime Customs Service was born out of the opium wars, and the disruption of foreign

---

81 Jamieson, G., *Chinese Family and Commercial Law*, Shanghai, Kelly & Walsh, 1921.

82 Coates, *op. cit.*, 240. He made a complete recovery and went on later to teach at Beijing University.

trade which arose from the hostilities during the Taiping revolution when local Chinese officials were unable, or unwilling, to collect maritime trade and other taxes. However, unlike the Consular Service, the Maritime Customs was a department of the Chinese Government from its inception in Shanghai in 1854 until its demise as it was then structured in 1949. Over the years, the Service assumed responsibility for the management of domestic customs, the lighting of waterways, the postal service and anti-smuggling operations along the China coast and on the Yangzi. Latterly, the Service became involved in negotiations for foreign loans to China (since most were secured wholly, or in part, against Customs revenue) and in currency reform. The Service also represented Chinese interests at overseas trade and other exhibitions.

Often referred to as the Foreign Legion of the Far East, the Service employed a wide range of nationalities mainly as "outdoor staff" such as tidewaiters and marine surveyors. Writing in 1905 one contemporary remembered they included men from every imaginable stratum of society; "remittance men, drunks and sober men, gentlemen and rascals, ignorant and highly educated men. Love of adventure had attracted some of them to the Service; others were probably fugitives from justice; and some ... had joined from necessity."[83]

The British predominated in senior management roles where they were normally supportive of wider British interests in China. Recruitment to the examinations for "indoor staff", as they were known, was by way of nomination by the Inspector General of the Service, following recommendations from "Old China Hands", retired customs staff and the like. Newspaper advertisements were never used. The objective was to recruit good "chaps", preferably with a public school background, who would share the same social values as those recruited to the China Consular Service.[84]

During its formative period, the wily Scots-Irishman, Robert Hart, was Inspector General of the Customs Service from 1863 till his retirement in 1910. When appointed, he was responsible for seven ports. When he retired, the Service operated nearly forty customs houses across the

---

83 Rassmussen, A. H., *China Trader,* London, Constable and Company, 1954, 16.

84 Brunero, D., *Britain's Imperial Cornerstone in China*, Abingdon, Routeledge, 2006, 42-43.

country. At that time, Hart had a staff of some twelve thousand people and was responsible for raising a third of the Chinese Government's annual revenue.[85]

A number of Scots were recruited to administrative and professional posts in the Service and some were promoted to senior positions. A confidante of Hart, James Duncan Campbell from Edinburgh headed the Service's London Office for thirty four years from 1873 until his death in 1907. Probably one of the most influential officers during these years, he acted as Hart's *alter ego* in Europe where he was responsible for liaising with the British Foreign Office and other diplomatic missions. He personally screened personnel seeking senior appointments in the Service as well as procuring supplies which ranged from lighthouse apparatus to new vessels for the Chinese northern fleet.[86] On the other hand, John Clark Johnston from Perthshire had a more conventional career, serving in a number of ports across China, and finally as Commissioner of Customs successively in Yichang, Ningbo and Beihai. By contrast, the first six years of William MacDonald's service in China were spent at university in Beijing teaching English. He later became Vice-President and Dean of the Customs College in the capital. His family came from Dingwall.

David Crawford Dick from Edinburgh, and Lawrence Tweedie-Stodart from Tweedsmuir, both trained with D. & C. Stevenson, Engineers to the Scottish Lighthouse Board, before taking up appointments with the Maritime Customs. They were involved in the modernisation of coastal lights including the installation of improved optical equipment and burners. During his time as Engineer-in-Chief of the Service, Dick oversaw the construction of Chilang Point lighthouse on Daya Bay (Bias Bay) which, at the time of construction in 1911, was one of the most powerful lights in the world. The Stevensons would have been proud!

As we have seen, Scottish trained doctors, like Patrick Manson, also sought appointment with the Service as port doctors. Unlike the Army Medical Service, or the Indian Medical Service, port doctors did not have to sit competitive entry examinations, or undertake mandatory

---

85 The Hart family connection with the Service continued when his nephew, Frederick Maze, served as Inspector General from 1929 to 1943.

86 Campbell, R. S., *James Duncan Campbell; A Memoir by his Son*, Cambridge, Massachusetts, Harvard University Press, 1970, 39 - 40.

preparatory courses. Additionally, as a port doctor, there were many opportunities for financially lucrative private medical work, as well as opportunities to study new forms of disease, as Manson indeed did.[87]

Another Scottish doctor, Halliday Macartney from Kirkcudbrightshire, had an usual career in China. Graduating from Edinburgh University in 1858, he joined the Army Medical Service and worked for four years in China before resigning in order to become more involved with local affairs. He became a confidante of Li Hongzhang, a rising star in the Imperial civil service. With Li's support, and drawing on his knowledge of chemistry as a student, Macartney established an arsenal to make western style munitions, first, at Songjiang, near Shanghai, then at Suzhou and, eventually, at Nanjing where he remained in charge until 1875.

Following the Margary incident in 1875, when a British official was murdered in China, and the Chefoo Convention of the following year, a representative of the Imperial Government was appointed in London. With his knowledge of the Chinese language, and Chinese affairs, plus connections in Britain, Macartney was the ideal candidate to organize the Chinese mission. He was appointed, successively, Counsellor and then English Secretary to the Chinese legation, representing Chinese interests, not just in Britain but across Europe as well, until his retirement in 1906.

His obituary in the *British Medical Journal* was generous. "Probably none of the British officials who have served the Chinese Government had more influence than the ex-army doctor who combined the native shrewdness of the Scot with the acquired talent for negotiation of the Chinese."[88] On his part, Macartney was more modest. "I flatter myself that my efforts have not been altogether unsuccessful," he wrote in 1899, "and to this must be imputed the abandonment of the gunboat action and the more respectful language which our ministers and our consuls have been taught to use in addressing Chinese officials - language more compatible with the growth of friendly relations between the two

---

87 Haynes, D. M., *Imperial Medicine: Patrick Manson and the conquest of tropical disease,* Philadelphia, University of Pennsylvania Press, 2001, 20.
88 *British Medical Journal,* June 16 1906, 1442-44.

countries, and the conservation of the cups and saucers of the Yamen." (Chinese Government office).[89]

Scots involvement in public administration was not restricted to the Consular Service, the Maritime Customs or work with the Imperial Government. Their wider role in Hong Kong, and elsewhere in China, is demonstrated in the remarkable careers of James Stewart Lockhart, and Reginald Johnston, both of whom shared similar interests and worked together, first in Hong Kong, and then in the remote British colony of Weihaiwei in eastern Shandong Province.

Administrator, sinologist, Confucian scholar, James Stewart Lockhart was born in Argyll in 1858 into a family with historic Jacobite connections. After studying at George Watson's College in Edinburgh, he went to Edinburgh University in 1874 to study Greek and English literature. After two failed attempts to join the Indian Civil Service, he was successful in securing a post in Hong Kong where he arrived in late 1879.[90]

A talented linguist, he progressed quickly through the ranks, eventually becoming Registrar General, a post that also carried with it the title of Protector of Chinese which brought him into contact with a wide range of local individuals and issues. Through his involvement in organizations like the Tung Wah Hospital Group, established in 1870 to promote the practice of Chinese medicine in Hong Kong, and the District Watch Committee, formed in 1866 to guard property in predominantly Chinese housing areas of the colony, he came to understand the aspirations, and thinking, of Chinese people who were all but excluded from the governmental process at that time. More importantly, non-European community leaders, like He Qi (Kai Ho Kai), who was a contemporary, and graduate of Aberdeen University, became firm friends. At a time when racial distinctions were emphasised, Stewart Lockhart and his wife entertained widely, welcoming to their home on the Peak people from different racial backgrounds.[91]

---

89 Crichton-Browne, J., *The Life of Sir Halliday Macartney*, London, John Lane, 1908, 482-83.

90 Stewart Lochart did not graduate from Edinburgh University.

91 Airlie, S., *Thistle and Bamboo*, Hong Kong, Oxford University Press, 1989, 57.

Stewart Lockhart was not the first, and certainly not the last, Hong Kong Government officer to have a very high opinion of his own importance and abilities. He twice applied for the top government post of colonial secretary before finally achieving this prize in 1895. He expected to be subsequently appointed as Governor of Hong Kong but was to be disappointed. In his rapid rise to power, he had made good friends but also powerful enemies. Moreover, it seems the Colonial Office was mindful of the claims of other senior personnel who might be better qualified for the post of Governor because of their experience elsewhere – even if they could not speak a word of Chinese.

During his seven years as colonial secretary, the focus of much of his work was the management of the area adjacent to Hong Kong which had been leased to Britain for ninety nine years following the Convention of Beijing in 1898. A beautiful part of southern Guangdung Province, the nine hundred square kilometres were home to small farmers and fishermen with proud ancestral traditions. Stewart Lockhart threw himself into the task of integrating the New Territories, as they became known, into Hong Kong, surveying what was there, setting up a locally focused administration and reaching out to the community which regarded its new landlord with a mixture of amusement and disdain.

At the same time as Britain acquired the New Territories for Hong Kong, Weihaiwei on the coast of Shandong Province was also leased. Fearful of Japanese and Russian ambitions in the area, the intention was to develop Weihaiwei into the Gibraltar of the Yellow Sea, providing a base, and coaling station, for the Royal Navy. With his linguistic skills, and recent experience in the New Territories, Stewart Lockhart was the obvious choice as the first civil commissioner - he arrived in Weihaiwei in May 1902.

Like Scotland's Southern Uplands, the gentle rolling countryside around Weihaiwei would have reminded Stewart Lockhart of home. Though bitterly cold in winter, the climate was mild for much of the year and certainly less enervating than humid Hong Kong. Stewart Lockhart busied himself setting up his office at Port Edward and, with very limited financial resources, establishing a paternalistic, non-invasive form of local government for the hundred and fifty thousand inhabitants of Britain's then newest colony. However, despite his best efforts,

Weihaiwei never became the prosperous trading centre that had been envisaged. Other priorities meant that the naval infrastructure was never fully maximised on Liugong Island; commercial port development was frustrated by opposition from the Chinese and the Germans in Shandong Province; and inward investment from Hong Kong and Shanghai never materialised because of serious doubts about the long term future of the colony. Investors were concerned that Britain might return Weihaiwei to China as indeed happened in 1930.

Stewart Lockhart enjoyed excellent relations with successive Governors of Shandong Province who clearly respected his sensitive approach and scholarship. Operating, as he did, in a cultural context so different from that of Hong Kong, he was, however, increasingly seen by the Colonial Office as an eccentric. More dangerously, it was felt he was "too close" to the little colony, and the people, he governed – always anathema for the prospects of a British colonial administrator wherever he worked. Although knighted in 1908, his promotion prospects evaporated and he remained in Weihaiwei for the rest of his career. He is remembered today as an enlightened administrator who sought to understand, and do his best for, the community for which he was responsible, He was fortunate in having as his colleague, and friend, another Scot, Reginald Johnston from Edinburgh, who shared many of his enthusiasms and interests.

Johnston spend most of his life travelling, first, to escape an abusive father in Edinburgh from where he made his way to study at Cambridge; he then travelled to Hong Kong and Wehaiwei to avoid the disgrace of being associated with his dysfunctional family when his father was found to be bankrupt after his death. But he made other journeys as well. Rather than return to Britain on home leave, he travelled through China, Tibet and Myanmar – an adventure he later wrote about in *From Peking to Mandalay* published in 1908. This journey spawned others both physical and spiritual. Encountering different religious traditions on his travels, he began a lifelong study of Buddhism which was to empower much of his life and thinking.

Johnston worked in Hong Kong until 1906 when he moved to Weihaiwei. As Stewart Lockhart's assistant, he acquired an intimate knowledge of the local community there. Johnston's recollections of this strangest of British colonies are recorded in his delightful *Lion and Dragon in Northern China* which he dedicated to Stewart Lockhart.

If Johnston was regarded by his British colleagues as something of a religious crank, clearly beyond the pale, his talents had not gone unnoticed elsewhere. His sensitivities to Chinese affairs, his linguistic abilities, and knowledge of China, had come to the attention of Li Jingmai, a former diplomat who had the ear of President Xu Shichang. After informal consultation, Johnston was offered the post of tutor to the former Emperor, Puyi, who was then thirteen years old. Johnston held the post for six years, recalling his time at Court in his *Twilight in the Forbidden City* which provides a unique insight into Chinese life and politics at that time. Subsequently, Johnston was Commissioner in Weihaiwei from 1927 until 1930 when the colony was returned to China.

If the engagement of Stewart Lockhart and Johnston with China had been respectful, based on a search for cultural understanding, the experience of other Scots was less so arising, as it did, from military deployment, during periods when western and Chinese interests were in conflict.

Scottish regiments of the British Army served in China from the early days of British intervention right through till 1997 when China resumed sovereignty in Hong Kong. They fought against Chinese troops in the first and second Anglo-Chinese Wars, during the Boxer rising and against the Japanese in the defence of Hong Kong in 1941. Otherwise, they were almost always deployed in protecting British interests and in support of the civil authorities in Hong Kong, Shanghai and elsewhere in China.

Scots also played a role in law enforcement agencies in China, particularly the Hong Kong Police Force and the Shanghai Municipal Police.

Like most colonial police forces, the Hong Kong Police, established in 1844 quickly assumed a public order role in order to maintain the new social order imposed on the colony and uphold the *pax britannica*. Lawlessness was rife, and the infant law enforcement agency struggled to combat a raft of problems ranging from piracy to prostitution. One of the main problems facing the newly appointed Commissioner, Charles May, was the difficulty in recruiting suitable people as constables. As most local Chinese residents of Hong Kong detested their new masters, recruits were often soldiers discharged from British regiments, or drawn from the European flotsam and jetsam of the China coast, some of whom were Scots. Because of the traditional Chinese practice of "squeeze", corruption was rife such that, in 1871, a sizeable number of constables were dismissed and replaced, in part, by a group of Scots policemen from Edinburgh.

Throughout the colonial period of its history, the ethnic composition of the Force was a matter of concern.[92] Until the late 1940s, the majority of constables were Sikhs recruited from India, to where many returned after partition and independence in 1947. Thereafter, local Chinese started to join, soon making up three quarters of the establishment. However, expatriate numbers remained high – in 1990 some sixty per cent of the five hundred senior posts in the Force were held by expatriates, most of them British, many of them Scots.

The only Scots Commissioner of the Force was Duncan William Mackintosh. Between 1946 and 1953, he managed the reorganization of the Force after the Japanese occupation, focusing on creating better working conditions, and pay, for junior officers as well as making a start to building Police living quarters. He is remembered for the distinctive look-out posts, known as Mackintosh Cathedrals, developed along the Hong Kong – China border to counter illegal immigration. The Hong Kong Police Band, complete with pipers, wears the Mackintosh tartan in his memory.

The other Police Force in China, which employed a significant number of Scots, was that of Shanghai. The Force was established by the Municipal Council in 1854 to police the Shanghai International Settlement. Largely British officered, the Force expanded during the nineteenth century to include Chinese and Sikh personnel and, later, nationals from Japan and Russia. Policing Shanghai was a dangerous, and demanding, task which called for bravery and judgement, even if the latter was sometimes lacking. The May Thirtieth Movement had its origins in the catastrophic policing failure in Nanjing Road in 1925 when

---

92 Deflem, M., Featherstone, R., Li, Yunqing and Sutph, S., in *Policing the Pearl; Historical Transformations of Law Enforcement in Hong Kong*, International Journal of Police Science and Management, 10 (3), 2008, 349-356.

Sikh and Chinese police opened fire, killing nine student demonstrators and injuring many others. Under the direction of William E. Fairbairn, and Eric A. Sykes, the Shanghai Police pioneered innovative close combat and pistol shooting techniques which were, later, to be taught to irregular forces at the British Secret Intelligence Services Special training centre at Inverailort House in Lochaber between 1940 and 1942 – a long way from Shanghai.

There were other Scottish connections as well. Three of Hong Kong's Governors in the twentieth century were Scots - Robert Black, Murray MacLehose and David Wilson – all of them holding office after 1945. Their position enabled them not only to influence events in Hong Kong but also to engage, in different ways, with China.

Educated at George Watson's College, and Edinburgh University, Robert Black was, perhaps, the last truly "colonial" Governor of Hong Kong. He joined the Colonial Service in 1930 and served in Trinidad, Malaya, North Borneo and Singapore before coming to Hong Kong in 1958 where he had previously been colonial secretary. He faced a myriad of problems during his six years as Governor, including a massive influx of refugees from the Chinese mainland fleeing the fallout from the Great Leap Forward. With nearly a million people squatting in filthy urban squalor, or on open hillsides, Black inaugurated a programme to alleviate the worst of the housing problems. But funds were scarce and there were other priorities including an acute water shortage – in 1960 water was rationed to three days a week. When his request for financial assistance to augment the housing programme was turned down, he publicly criticised the British Government, suggesting the situation he faced was like Glasgow being asked to absorb a million refugees and then find money to house them.[93]

A popular Governor with a Scottish focus on education, he was the driving force behind the revival of Hong Kong University, providing government capital funding for the reconstruction of facilities destroyed during the Japanese occupation, and increased finance for recurrent costs. Although he is remembered today through the Sir Robert Black College of Education, a constituent part of Hong Kong University, perhaps his greatest achievement was to persuade a disparate group of oth-

---

93 *The Guardian*, London, 23 November 1999.

er educational institutions to combine together in 1963 to form a new Chinese language university, the Chinese University of Hong Kong, which was developed on a spectacular, green field site near Sha Tin in the New Territories.

Seven years after Robert Black retired in 1964 another Scot, Murray MacLehose, took over as Governor of Hong Kong. MacLehose was different in that he came from a Foreign Office, rather than Colonial Service, background. One of the most able Scotsmen of his generation, MacLehose was to play a momentous role in Hong Kong's history.

The colony's longest serving Governor, MacLehose laid the foundations of the territory's prosperity and stability, whilst facilitating the opening up of China in the aftermath of the Cultural Revolution. Overcoming the problems confronting him as Governor called for guts, tenacity and resolve. He had all three qualities and not a few others as well.

Fluent in Chinese, his strong practical bent kept him in touch with the reality others preferred to ignore. A visionary, with a passionate agenda to improve the lot of ordinary Hong Kong people, he knew the devil was in the detail and insisted on mastering it. Never one to suffer fools gladly, (and there were many in Hong Kong), he knew when to back-off politically and pocket what had been achieved. A large man physically, he cut an impressive figure striding through the miserable squatter settlements, or sparkling new towns which replaced them in the countryside near the Chinese border.

Stories of his courage and perseverance abounded. Working with Chinese guerrilla forces behind enemy lines during the war, he strode into the bar of the Japanese-controlled club at Shantou (Swatow), signed for a gin and tonic, swigged it down, and walked out! Not a few civil servants quailed at the return from Government House of their carefully drafted, finely worded proposals, over which was scrawled; "Not good enough – must be sorted out now", and the ubiquitous, or so it seemed, big "M" in red ink. Murray MacLehose was determined to make a difference.

He took over a complacent, expatriate-led civil service that had changed little since Victorian times. He brought in American management consultants and radically restructured it, encouraging the promotion of bright, young Chinese. At the same time, he gradually increased local representation on the colony's Legislative Council to ensure community concerns were readily addressed.

Corruption in the public and private sectors was endemic and he tackled it head-on. The police mutinied, but he stood firm. Once known as the best police force money could buy, the Hong Kong Police went on to become one of the cleanest, and most efficient, in Asia. Waves of refugees, and years of under spending, had left hundreds of thousands of families living in insanitary, flimsy wooden, oil cloth and corrugated iron squatter huts which were regularly washed away in the summer typhoon rains. He breathed life into a fledgling housing programme which took off at a frantic pace. Within twenty years over two million people had been rehoused in bright, modern homes.

A quintessential Scot, who enjoyed Burns and St Andrew's Nights, he insisted Hong Kong should have its own focus for art and music. In typical MacLehose style, an arts centre was rapidly built on reclaimed land beside the harbour. The tar was still warm on the access road when he came to the opening concert.

MacLehose knew that Hong Kong's future was implacably tied to that of China. With Maoist fundamentalism coming to the end on the Chinese mainland, he sensed there were advantages, both to China and Hong Kong, in looking to the future rather than the past. The first Hong Kong Governor to visit Beijing since the Second World War, he met Deng Xiaoping in March 1979. Back in Hong Kong, he relayed Deng's message that investors "should set their hearts at ease". Confidence soared. Hong Kong would play a key role in the modernisation of southern China and beyond.

MacLehose had his faults. He was often abrasive and rude. His zeal to push forward major building projects frequently outstripped the capacity of the construction industry. Commuters living in new towns got used to years of travelling misery until the transport infrastructure caught up with the housing-led development. He took rapid likes and dislikes, and was not always the best judge of ability or character. He could have accelerated the process of democratising the territory's political institutions but, perhaps, was persuaded that the preference then in Hong Kong, and China, was for dollars not votes. Hong Kong people did not lavish affection on MacLehose but they respected the big, dour Scot whose legacy was a prosperous, modern Hong Kong in a dynamic and changing China.

Hong Kong's last Scottish Governor, Wilson, was described by a veteran Hong Kong journalist as a "reserved, scholarly figure, with an assertive wife". Although he had been closely involved through the Foreign Office with the formulation of British policy *vis a vis* China and Hong Kong, he was seen by some of his peers as not having the sort of charisma, and political weight, that might have carried Hong Kong further along the path to a comfortable transition to Chinese rule.[94] It seems their reservations were not unfounded. Appointed in 1987, it was expected Wilson would be the colony's last British Governor – a historic role which was denied him.

His governorship faced many challenges. Significantly, in the run up to China's resumption of sovereignty, many younger, local politicians had come to believe that Hong Kong's future could best be secured by the British developing credible, democratic institutions in the colony before they departed - as had happened elsewhere when British rule ended. Many were harshly critical of the slow pace of democratisation. However, it was Wilson's successor, Chris Patten, who publicly championed local concerns about democracy. Patten emphasised that Hong Kong's unique position in Asia was based on the freedoms enjoyed by its people – freedoms which have, in fact, remained largely unchanged since 1997. Widely rumoured to have been moved on by John Major, and the Conservative Government in London, Wilson left the colony in 1992 with a peerage. He was later appointed Chairman of the utility company, Scottish Hydro-Electric plc.

Whatever their record, or area of engagement in public life in China, Scots, by and large, brought with them an openness to the problems of the day and a determination to try to bring them to a conclusion. The outcomes they achieved were often misunderstood, or wrong, but their

---

94 Spurr, R., *Excellency; The Governors of Hong Kong*, Hong Kong, Form/Asia, 1995, 246; Piers Jacobs, *The Last "Colonial" Financial Secretary,* in Blyth, S. and Wotherspoon, I., *Hong Kong Remembers,* Hong Kong, Oxford University Press, 1996, 220-21.

directness, coupled in many cases with a genuine concern about the society in which they lived, played an important part in the evolution of administrative and other structures, in China. Certainly, in proportion to their numbers, these Scots in public service in China kicked well above their height – and left behind them not a few outstanding achievements.

6 Chinese Lads o' Pairts

Western learning for practical application.

ZHANG ZHIDONG.

On a bright summer's morning in 1855, a young student made his way from his lodgings near the Cowgate in Edinburgh, up through High School Yards, past the city's infirmary, and on to what was then known popularly as the "Tounis College", the University of Edinburgh. There, later in the day, he was awarded the degree of Doctor of Medicine (MD).

His journey had been short, but it marked the end of a longer one. The student, whose name was Huang Kuan (Wong Fun), had come from China to study medicine in Edinburgh and was the first Chinese to be awarded a degree in western medicine by any European, university. His presence amongst the happy group of new graduates was important because it highlighted the growth, and increasing diversity, of the encounters then developing between Scotland's universities and students from abroad.

Students came to Scotland's universities from a variety of backgrounds. Many local students were from poor families who scraped together enough money to pay their fees and lodgings. Blessed with brains, and burning with ambition, they became known as "lads o' pairts" – young men of talent and ability. Although Scotland's universities were uniquely national institutions, often seen as the guardians of Scottish culture, they had always been receptive to students and scholars from beyond their walls, particularly those who came from "furth o' Scotland", including China.[95]

Students from abroad came to study in Scotland's universities because of their liberal entrance policies, academic standing, particularly in medicine, and close association with many of the leading figures of the internationally recognised artistic, cultural and intellectual advances of the Scottish Enlightenment. Through them, the universities nurtured attitudes, ideas and professional practices which would, as Arthur Herman has suggested, promote nothing less than "the basic institutions, ideas, attitudes and habits of mind that characterise the modern age."[96]

The universities' deepening engagement with the overseas world called for them to encompass a student body drawn from diverse backgrounds, embrace new academic fields of interest, and adapt to changing employment demands overseas. Since the transmission, and modification, of knowledge and cultural values is never entirely a one-way process, Scotland's universities were, in turn, influenced by their exposure to events and ideas emanating from other parts of the world. In a real sense, Scotland's universities served the international community and benefited from the multicultural exposure it provided.

A small but significant number of Chinese students came to study in Scotland in the tumultuous century between the Taiping revolution and the inauguration of the People's Republic. They came at a time of unprecedented change in China, when internal pressures combined with external forces to create a dynamic situation politically, economically and socially. In the heady political atmosphere that preceded the disintegration of the Qing dynasty, a number of educational initiatives were launched, many of which sought to promote, using Zhang Zhidong's famous phrase, "Chinese learning for the fundamental principles, western

---

95 Falconer, R. A., *Scottish Influence in the Higher Education of Canada* in *Royal Society of Canada, Proceedings and Transactions,* Third Series, Vol. 21, Ottawa, 1927, 20.
96 Herman, A., *The Scottish Enlightenment*, London, Fourth Estate, 2002, 9–10.

learning for practical application."[97] The demands of balancing the material benefits of western science and technology with the maintenance of traditional values, and a Chinese identity, gave rise to tensions which hastened, and at the same time impeded, China's modernisation throughout the twentieth century.[98]

The newly found interest in western learning and science manifested itself in the growing number of Chinese students who went overseas to Japan, the United States and Europe for technical and university-level education. It has been estimated that, of the Chinese students who went abroad to study between 1903 and 1919, some forty two per cent studied in Japan, thirty four per cent in the United States and twenty four per cent in Europe.[99]

Admiration for the successes of the Meiji restoration, coupled with close geographic proximity and lower study costs, made Japan an obvious choice, even if students from China often railed against the close supervision meted out by the Japanese authorities. Schools and colleges established by American Protestant missionaries, such as the Canton Christian College (later Lingnan University), served as feeders for universities and colleges in North America. Chinese students of the period also studied in Europe, particularly in France, where many empathised with the political values of the French Revolution. However, although Britain was deeply involved in Chinese economic and political life, it had little direct interest in educational matters and this is reflected in the comparatively small number of students who chose to study there.

The Scottish universities sought to facilitate the admission of Chinese students by, for example, in the case of Edinburgh, agreeing that the Chinese language might be substituted as an alternative to Latin and Greek in the joint preliminary entrance examinations.[100] Many of these

---

97 Lutz, J. G., *China and the Christian Colleges, 1850-1950*, Ithaca & London, Cornell University Press, 1971, 82.

98 Hayhoe, R., *China's Universities, 1895-1995*, New York & London, Garland, 1996, 29.

99 Hsu, I. C. Y., *The Rise of Modern China*, New York & London, Oxford University Press, 4th edn. 1990, 496.

100 University of Edinburgh, *Edinburgh University Calendar, 1913–14*, Edinburgh, James Thin, 1913, 84.

students had earlier studied at the newly established national universities in China, such as the Imperial University of Beijing founded in 1898, or Shanxi University founded in 1902, at one of the Christian missionary institutions, such as the Baptist College and Seminary in Shanghai, or, indeed, elsewhere abroad. For many, their time in Scotland provided an opportunity to familiarise themselves at first hand with different aspects of western science and technology. He Qi, for example, graduated MBCM from Aberdeen in 1879 and went on to play a formative role in public life in Hong Kong.[101] H. C. Yu was awarded a BSc in Pure Science by Edinburgh University in 1910 and later worked in the civil service of the Chinese Republic. A member of the Chinese Academy of Sciences, the geologist Ren Mei'e (Jen Mei-ngo) was awarded a PhD by Glasgow University in 1939 for his work on the morphological evolution of Clydesdale and its neighbouring regions.

Many students were later able to apply the knowledge and skills they had acquired in Scotland on their return to China, where, as the economic infrastructure was developed, they found openings as academics, entrepreneurs and managers. Some, like Ding Wenjiang (Ting Wen-chiang) who took a BSc in Geology, Geography and Zoology at Glasgow University in 1911, were outstanding scientists, widely recognised both at home and abroad. Ding was, as Charlotte Furth has rightly noted, perhaps one of the best known of the few pioneer western-trained scientists in China during the early years of the Chinese Republic.[102]

Ding's seven years as a student in Britain vividly illuminate the forces which influenced young Chinese students to consider studying abroad and the educational and social challenges they faced whilst overseas. An able and articulate student from a wealthy land-owning family in Jiangsu Province, Ding first went abroad to study in Japan in 1902. His decision to come to study in Scotland was prompted by a circular letter from Wu Zhihui, who was then studying at Edinburgh University. Wu believed that, in comparison with Japan, where he suggested Chinese students ate Chinese food, talked about Chinese politics and didn't

---

101 Choa, G. H., *The Life and Times of Sir Kai Ho Kai*, Hong Kong, Chinese University Press, 1981, 101–24.

102 Furth, C., *Ting Wen-chiang*, Cambridge, Massachusetts, Harvard University Press, 1970, 5.

study, Edinburgh offered real opportunities to absorb authentic western learning at moderate cost. Described by Marilyn Levine as one of the giants of modern Chinese education, Wu was a prominent supporter of the work–study movement abroad and was later to play a leading role in promoting anarchism in China.[103]

With two friends, Ding arrived in Britain in the summer of 1904 and made his way to Edinburgh to meet Wu. To his horror, he found Wu penniless and realised that his financial calculations for living in Scotland on six hundred yuan a year were unrealistic. Whilst Wu headed west to seek work at Glasgow's docks, Ding was befriended by a former medical missionary in China who arranged for him to attend a local school in Lincolnshire. From there he went to Cambridge two years later, but the cost was beyond his budget and he withdrew. After some time travelling on the continent, he settled in Glasgow where he enrolled at the University there in 1908.[104]

Ding's career owed much to his stay in Glasgow. On his return to China, he vigorously applied his western-acquired skills as a geologist with considerable success. By 1914, he had been appointed head of China's newly established Geological Survey. But his career was not confined solely to exploration and research. Until his untimely death in 1936, he was involved in a range of activities which embraced journalism, business management, scholarship and politics in which he sought to explicate, for a society still enthralled by Confucian values, the potential benefits of applying scientific methodology to areas of intellectual and national endeavour which, hitherto, had not been explored in this way.

Although most Chinese students attended courses with a scientific focus, a few came to Scotland to study philosophy, political economy and western literature. Some were to distinguish themselves in literature and politics after they returned home.

---

103 Levine, M. A., *The Found Generation: Chinese Communists in Europe during the Twenties*, Seattle & London, University of Washington Press, 1993, 24, 28–32; Bailey, P. J., *Reform the People: Changing Attitudes towards Popular Education in Early Twentieth-Century China*, Edinburgh, Edinburgh University Press, 1990, 228–30.
104 Furth, *op. cit.*, 23–25.

Originally from Penang in the Straits Settlements, one of the first Chinese scholars to study in Scotland was Gu Hongming, who graduated MA from Edinburgh in 1877. A talented administrator and linguist, Gu served as Zhang Zhidong's secretary before teaching European literature at Beijing University. Regarded as the leader of the conservative group of the New Culture Movement (May Fourth Movement), he was appointed Principal of Shandong University shortly before his death in 1928. Yang Changji, remembered for his influence on the young Mao Zedong, studied philosophy at Aberdeen, where he was awarded an MA in 1912. Returning to China, he took up a teaching appointment at Changsha in Hunan Province where he first taught Mao. It was largely because of Yang's influence as a newly appointed professor at Beijing University that Mao secured the post of librarian's assistant there in 1918.[105]

Other Chinese thinkers and writers who embraced the New Culture Movement also studied in Scotland. Writer and revolutionary Zhang Shizhao studied political economy at Edinburgh University between 1908 and 1911 where he appears to have become enamoured with the political theories of Walter Bagehot and other liberal British social scientists.[106] He used the *Tiger Magazine*, first published in 1914, to promote his views, which sought to interpret foreign democratic ideas and institutions in a Chinese context.[107]

In response to the difficulties in establishing western medical teaching facilities in China, Scottish-trained medical practitioners, most of them missionaries, probably influenced a number of Chinese students to study medicine in Scotland in this period. Perhaps more so than elsewhere in Asia, the problems of introducing western medical education to China were fraught with cultural sensitivities and logistical obstacles. Western-trained missionaries led the way with medical classes held in locations such as the Canton Missionary Hospital and St. Luke's Hospital

---

105 Schram, S. R., *The Political Thought of Mao Tse-Tung*, New York, Praeger, 1963, 12–14.

106 Chow, Tse-tsung, *The May Fourth Movement*, Cambridge, Massachusetts and London, Harvard University Press, 1960, 43.

107 Wang, Y. C., *Chinese Intellectuals and the West, 1872–1949*, Chapel Hill, University of North Carolina Press, 1966, 342.

in Shanghai. Standards, however, varied considerably and the number of students completing their studies was very small indeed. Scottish-trained medical graduates, such as Huang Kuan and James Cantlie, who would later become the first President of the Royal Society of Tropical Medicine, played an important role in the early development of western medical education in China.

Demand, however, far outstripped supply, and funds for books, equipment and adequate teaching facilities were almost always limited.[108] The China Medical Missionary Association, established in 1886, took a leading role in promoting western medical education in China together with missionary and philanthropic groups in Britain, the United States and elsewhere. Although the development of medical education was boosted after 1915 by the efforts of the China Medical Board of the Rockefeller Foundation and the establishment of first-rank medical schools, such as the Union Medical College in Beijing, medical students from China continued to seek undergraduate and postgraduate medical qualifications and experience abroad, some of them in Scotland, throughout the life of the Chinese Republic.[109]

In the years following the end of the First World War, Chinese scholars of note enrolled in courses in the liberal arts in Scottish universities. The philosopher Zhu Guangqian, who made a significant contribution to the development of modern Chinese aesthetics, studied at Edinburgh University, where he was awarded an MA in 1928. The poet and translator Wang Xindi studied English literature at Edinburgh University from 1936 to 1938, making the acquaintance, amongst others, of T.S. Eliot and Stephen Spender.

The growth in the number of Chinese students in Scotland in this period can be attributed, in part, to the decision by the British Government (following the example of the US Government) to waive its claim to the outstanding portion of the reparations due from China as a result of the 1900 Boxer rising. In arrangements concluded with the Chinese authorities in 1930, it was agreed that the remaining funds should be applied as development capital for enterprises in China, and that the

---

108 Balme, H., *China and Modern Medicine*, London, Church Missionary Society, 1921, 57–59.
109 Balme, *op. cit.*, 119–22.

interest arising would be used for educational and cultural purposes. Towards this end, twenty competitive, annual scholarships were established for study in the United Kingdom. Although a number of Chinese students continued to finance their study in Britain by other means, the new scholarships certainly boosted interest in studying in Britain, as well as student numbers, which increased from fifty five in 1932 to one hundred and eighty seven in 1943.[110]

As well as taking courses at the undergraduate level in arts, medicine and science, students from China also studied for postgraduate qualifications. Between 1916 and 1961, for example, three hundred and forty six Chinese students successfully completed doctoral dissertations in Britain, of whom forty seven (13.6%) obtained their degrees from Scottish universities.[111] Of those studying in Scotland, over three-quarters attended Edinburgh University, which awarded forty one doctorates to Chinese students in this period. In the wider British context, Edinburgh was clearly an important study centre for students from China. After Cambridge and the London School of Economics, Edinburgh was third in respect of the number of postgraduate degrees awarded in this period. Almost two-thirds (64.1%) of Chinese postgraduate students coming to Britain studied science, particularly chemistry, civil engineering and physics. The profile for those studying in Scotland is broadly similar, with nearly three-quarters (74.4%) of postgraduates studying science. Six Chinese students were awarded doctorates in medicine between 1916 and 1961, all of them at the University of Edinburgh. The range of liberal arts PhD research topics was extensive. Partially mirroring the political interests of the time, they focused on economic and political relations between China and Britain.

The growth of the Chinese student community throughout the 1920s and '30s led to the formation of associations of Chinese students in the Scottish universities. Through the efforts of Dugald Christie, the medical missionary who had served in Shenyang, a Sino-Scottish Society was formed at Edinburgh University in 1929. A Sino-Scottish Student

---

110 Wang, *op. cit.*, 140–41, 513.

111 The data in this paragraph is extrapolated by the author from Yuan, Tung-li, *Doctoral Dissertations by Chinese Students in Great Britain and Northern Ireland, 1916–1961*, in *Chinese Culture*, Taipei?, Vol. 4, No. 4, 1963, 107–37.

Society had been formed earlier at Glasgow University in 1913. These associations had the common aim of promoting the interests of their members, integrating them into the communities in which they lived and providing a forum in which Chinese culture and society could be portrayed.

As with other groups of foreign students, the outbreak of hostilities in 1939 led to a reduction in the number of new students from China coming to Scotland. Thereafter, the inauguration of the People's Republic in 1949 effectively stemmed for nearly a quarter of a century the flow of students coming to Scotland directly from China.

In seeking to inculcate aspects of western learning, Scotland's universities perhaps passed on something of the Scottish tradition of the democratic intellect which emphasised a unified, generalist approach to knowledge based on first principles. It may even be possible, as John Hargreaves has suggested, to identify specific instances where Scottish-taught ideas may have been carried over into Chinese thinking of the day. A case in point is the possible influence Hegelian idealism, taught by Professor Sir James Baillie at Aberdeen, had on Mao's intellectual mentor, Yang Changji.[112] But even if direct connections cannot be made, it is worth noting that the role of the Scottish universities in providing tertiary education for Chinese students was well recognised. Visiting Edinburgh University in 1943, the "Silent Traveller", the delightful Jiang Yi (Chiang Yee), was at pains to remind his hosts of the distinguished Chinese students who had passed through the "gloomy" portals of the Old College.[113]

Drawing on what they had learnt, Chinese graduates of Scotland's universities played a not insignificant part in the great drama that was unfolding in China in the years between 1850 and 1950. Their involvement in the changing society of their day is a pointed indicator of the international focus of Scottish higher education, which remains one of its distinguishing features.

Today, in a different cultural and political environment, students from all over China come to study in Scotland, following a path well-trodden by

---

112 Hargreaves, J. D., *Academe and Empire*, Aberdeen, Aberdeen University Press, 1994, 38.
113 Chiang Yee, *The Silent Traveller in Edinburgh*, London, Methuen, 1948, 128.

their countrymen whose pioneering presence in Scotland, and achievements in China, they can celebrate with much pride. In 2012, over six thousand students from China were studying in Scotland on a range of undergraduate and postgraduate courses. Moreover, Scottish universities have partnered with universities in China to export courses to be taught there, whilst Confucius Institutes, which aim to promote Chinese language and culture, have been established at Edinburgh, Glasgow and Strathclyde universities - testament indeed to a long, and tested, relationship between Scotland and China in the field of tertiary education.

7 Travels in Famed Cathay

Better fifty years of Europe than a cycle of Cathay.

The winter was already upon them when the Scottish Doctor, John Bell, and his party from St. Petersburg, finally approached Beijing. Entering the city through the great North Gate on 18 November 1720, accompanied by five hundred Chinese horsemen, was like entering another world. Earlier, the visitors had been excited to see the "much celebrated wall of China ... running from one high rock to another, with square towers at certain intervals ... (which) ... is most magnificent."[114] There were other surprises as well. "We were first entertained with tea, and a dram of hot arrack; after which supper was brought, and placed on the tables, without tablecloth, napkins, knives or forks. Instead of forks were laid down to every person a couple of ivory pins, with which the Chinese take up their meat."[115] Here was a society with different customs, other ways of doing business and alien traditions. Within a few weeks, Bell concluded "the behaviours of the Chinese is quite contrary to that of the Europeans." [116] His travelogue,

114 Bell, J., *Travels from St. Petersburg in Russia to various parts of Asia*, Vol.1, Edinburgh, W. Creech, 1788, 410
115 Bell, *op. cit.*, 418.
116 Bell, J., *Travels from St. Petersburg in Russia to various parts of Asia*, Vol. 2, Glasgow, R. & A. Foulis, 1788, 11.

published in 1753, enthralled the Scots of his day. Just over a century later, with easier access to the interior provided by the 1860 Convention of Beijing, his successors sought to further explore the country, and interpret Chinese society to avid readers at home.

Europeans like John Bell writing about China did so as a result of their experiences mainly as diplomats, government representatives or missionaries. However, by the end of the nineteenth century, a new type of traveller had emerged, one who did not necessarily have a direct employment, or vocational, connection with the places they visited whether that was China or elsewhere. Of course, writers from commercial, missionary and public service backgrounds, like Alexander Michie, Dugald Christie and Alexander Hosie still continued to provide insightful commentary on a changing China, but the independent travellers were often better able to catch some of the excitement, and drama, of visiting a new country and meeting its people for the first time. Their comments on the Chinese people they met, and the expatriates with whom they interacted, are frequently incisive and perceptive. Examples of such travellers with Scottish connections include Isabella Bird Bishop, Constance Frederica Gordon Cumming, the painter T. Hodgson Liddell, and the photographer John Thompson, all of whom visited China in the closing years of the nineteenth, or early in the twentieth, century.

As Elizabeth Hope Chang has noted, we cannot understand what nineteenth century commentators were writing about unless we also understand what they were looking at.[117] The images they formed of China were influenced by the political and religious thinking of the day, tempered by the commercial and political realities of trade and Empire. However, certain assumptions were usually taken as given – that the once great Celestial Empire was in decline, that western commercial initiatives might provide a way to reverse, or possibly inhibit, that process and that, if embraced, the ideas espoused by Christian missionaries might provide a secure basis for a new Chinese social order. Of course, within that broad framework, there was plenty of scope for individual, critical analysis and thought.

Doyenne of late Victorian women travellers, Isabella Bird Bishop recorded her impressions of China in *The Yangtze Valley and Beyond*

---

117 Chang, E. H., *Britain's Chinese Eye*, Stanford, Stanford University Press, 2010, 3.

which was published in 1899. She travelled throughout her life visiting, and writing about, locations as diverse as Hawaii, the Rocky Mountains, Japan, Korea and Morocco.

Originally from North Yorkshire, Isabella, first came to Scotland in 1860, following the death of her father, to live at 3 Castle Terrace, Edinburgh with her widowed mother, and sister Hennie. She quickly became involved in the issues of the day, visiting the Western Isles in 1861, and promoting measures to allow poverty stricken crofters to emigrate to North America. In 1869, she published *Notes on Old Edinburgh*, a searing criticism of the appalling slum housing conditions in the city. Three years earlier she had married Dr. John Bishop, who had been a resident surgeon at the city's Royal Infirmary and an assistant to Lister before going into private practice. They had a wide circle of friends amongst the *literati* of the city, including Professor John Stuart Blackie, Thomas Constable the printer and publisher and Noel Paton the artist. She was one of the founding members of the (Royal) Scottish Geographical Society in 1884. She died in Edinburgh in 1904.

A confident supporter of the multifaceted benefits of British imperialism, Bishop believed that Britain's role was to provide appropriate guidance, and support, for emergent China. She hoped this would preserve the integrity of this ancient civilization and neutralize what she thought were the rapacious efforts of other foreign powers intent on China's destruction. Whether China would develop or disintegrate she thought "depends very largely on the statesmanship and influence of Great Britain".[118]

Like other travellers of her generation, and since, she was fascinated by the mighty Yangzi and determined to explore as much of it as possible. Her journey was to take her from Shanghai, by way of the Grand Canal, to Hangzhou and then upriver by steamer to Yichang some one thousand six hundred kilometres from the coast. Before departing on a hired flat bottomed boat, she asked a local expatriate how she might pass her time as she sailed upriver. His reply was simple –"People have enough to do looking after their lives." Surviving the dangerous rapids, she made her way through the Three Gorges to the city of Wan Hsien (Wanxian). From there, she headed west by road to "the beyond", eventually reach-

---

118 Bishop, I. L. B., *The Yangtze Valley and Beyond*, London, John Murray, 1899, 544.

ing Somo home of the Mantze hill tribes who lived on the Chinese/ Tibetan border. She returned subsequently to the coast via Chongqing.

Bishop scorned the superficial and frivolous lifestyle of expatriates living in Shanghai, noting that many had never left the confines, and comforts, of this foreign concession to embrace the "real" China beyond. She was disappointed to find that many British traders could not speak Chinese and had to resort to the use of Pidgin English, or depend on the linguistic skills of intermediaries. By contrast, she noted that Japanese traders and clerks all spoke Chinese. With its fine buildings, well dressed men and women promenading on the bund, clubs, and polo races, Shanghai was dazzling – but it was not for her.[119] Her criticisms were not well received. *The Shanghai Mercury* commented "Heaven preserve you from your independent female globetrotter ... and a book where grammar, common-sense and truth are equally defiled. Oh! Miss Bird (Bishop), you and your class have a deal to answer for...."[120] So too had her critics.

Visiting Hangzhou at the start of her trip in 1896 she stayed with Dr. D. Duncan Main. Complete with its clock tower, she thought the CMS hospital which he had founded was one of the "great sights" of the city. Over fourteen thousand patients were treated every year, a remarkable achievement given the small number of trained staff available. She attributed the lack of hostility to foreigners in Hangzhou to the influence, and standing, of Dr. Main who was on amicable terms with local officials. One of the "crack mission hospitals of the East", it was paralleled only, in her view, by Dr. Christie's United Presbyterian mission hospital in Shenyang in north eastern China. Scottish trained doctors were clearly seen to be playing an important role in China.

Like most tourists before her, including Marco Polo, and after, Bishop marvelled at the beauty of Hangzhou's West Lake with its deep wooded bays and inlets, its forested hills, ravines, pagodas and pleasure boats. In the "glorious beauty of a Chinese spring" it was a perfect start to her journey – but the country through which she would be passing would little resemble what she remembered with such affection in Hangzhou,

119 Bishop, *op. cit.,* 17-21.
120 Dupee, J. N., *British Travel Writers in China – Writing Home to a British Public, 1890-1914,* New York, The Edwin Mellon Press, c 2004, 47.

"heaven below".[121] Wherever she went she attracted attention, not just as a foreigner, and a woman, but because of her large camera which she used to record the places, and some of the people, she met on her journey. In many instances, her grimy, sepia photographs were the first ever taken of the locations she visited and, indeed, helped to shape peoples' perceptions of China when later published in the west.

Travelling as she did was arduous and dangerous. The cry of "foreign devil" was never far from her ears; when sleeping in wayside inns, she was inevitably given the worst room, and once had to spend the night in a pigsty; crowds gathered to gape or, at worst, molest her – on one occasion she was knocked unconscious by a flying rock and was only saved from further injury by the arrival of soldiers despatched by the local Mandarin. Not surprisingly, she hated Chinese cities for their "incredible filth, indescribable odours, which ought to receive a strong Anglo-Saxon name, grime, forlornness, bustle, business and discordant noises…" Bishop was not, however, the ultra-critical foreign traveller as she has often been depicted. Chinese culture enthused her, from the stately buildings and temples she photographed to the "very clever" Chinese theatricals, performed without scenery, or a curtain, which she so enjoyed. She liked Chinese food and marvelled (as did the British fifty years later) at the wide variety of cuisine available. She respected the impoverished trackers (oarsmen) of her boat for "their honest work, pluck, endurance, hardihood, sobriety and good nature".

Like the majority of European travellers she abhorred the practice of women having their feet bound, but she thought Chinese women better than any others she had met in Asia. "They have plenty of good stuff in them and backbone. … They have much kindness of heart; they are very modest; they are faithful wives and … good mothers." Without corsets, waistbands or other constraints, she found Chinese women's attire so comfortable that she wore it from the start of her Chinese travels – she thought she might not take kindly to European dress when she had to wear it again![122]

Bishop wrote with verve. She was a shrewd and intelligent observer of what, for most, was an incomprehensible and strange society which she

---

121 Bishop, *op. cit.*, 44-48.
122 Bishop, *op. cit.* 331, 298, 159, 270, 242.

sought to explicate for an interested western audience. In this she was successful, in part, due to the uniqueness of her material. As Pat Barr has observed, "she told her tales well, she seldom retraced her steps, she never outstayed her welcome."[123]

By contrast, Thomas Hodgson Liddell's travels in China were far less extensive than Bishop's, and facilitated by his older brother who had "made good" in Shanghai. The younger son of an Edinburgh businessman, who ran a successful tanning business in the city's West Port, Liddell was one of many young artists influenced by the impressionist movement at the end of the nineteenth century. He specialised in landscape subjects, exhibiting at most of the major galleries. His better known works include *Brig O' Turk*, (1882) and *Ferryhouse on the Ouse* (1893). His family owned Liddell Brothers & Company Ltd. in Shanghai where they operated cotton mills and had other commercial interests. Liddell used these connections when he went to China "solely to paint pictures", writing about his experiences in *China, Its Marvel and Mystery* which was published in 1910.

Liddell went to a China that was certainly less tense than it had been in the years leading up to the Boxer rising when Bishop had visited. The western powers and Japan felt more in control of events in China, even if the demise of the Qing dynasty was imminent. Sikh policemen patrolled the streets of Hong Kong; large numbers of foreign troops were still stationed in and around Beijing – Liddell was delighted to find the Cameron Highlanders there – and communications with the wider world were much improved with new rail links to the major cities in Europe.

Liddell's trip took him from Hong Kong to Shanghai and most of the treaty ports. He was bowled over by Hong Kong. The view from the Peak "was altogether one of the most mysterious, fascinating and beautiful sights one can imagine."[124] He was welcomed to the Hong Kong Club and approved of the sort of good-fellowship he believed reigned in the East. "It is open house to all travellers and a most hearty welcome."[125] He painted in Hong Kong, Guangzhou and Shanghai

---

123 Barr, P., *A Curious Life for a Lady*, London, Macmillan, 1970, 340.

124 Liddell, T. H., *China, Its Marvel and Mystery*, New York, John Lane Company, 1910, 2.

125 Liddell, *op. cit.* 17.

where he was frequently the centre of attention from the passing crowds. Now with a "No 1 Boy" to manage his affairs, he travelled by house boat first to Suzhou and then to Hangzhou – it was all so new, interesting and fun! It was comfortable too as a large box of ice was sent from Shanghai to Hangzhou three times a week so whilst painting "I could always have a cool drink …"[126]

Leaving the summer heat of Shanghai, he visited Weihaiwei and then went on to Beidaihe (Pei Tai Ho) where many expatriates spent the summer months. In the autumn, he visited all the main tourist sites in Beijing, and the surrounding areas, including the Great Wall and the Ming Tombs. With the support of the British Legation, he was invited to paint in the Summer Palace and left one of his works to be displayed there. We do not know what became of that painting but some of his extant work, completed whilst in China, such as *Peking; The Llama Temple* (1909), provides an interesting, and colourful perspective, through the eyes of a Scottish painter, of Chinese life and landscape at the beginning of the twentieth century.

Although Liddell's experience in China was a very privileged one, he was a shrewd observer of people and postures. He believed that foreigners assumed too much authority in China and were not sensitive to local concerns. Taking in the atmosphere of a Shanghai tea house, he sensed that "from this little spot alone one could form a tolerably correct conception of the Chinese character, lovers of peace and beauty, and withal industrious and keen in business. Such in a nutshell is my estimate of the qualities possessed by the Chinese, qualities of which any nation might be proud…"[127] Shortly before leaving Beijing, he invited all his Chinese friends for dinner to thank them for their kindness and support. Each guest was given a special menu card on which he had painted some aspect of the Summer Palace.

Nearly thirty years before Liddell embarked on his painting expedition, a Scotswoman, also with an interest in painting, Constance Frederica Gordon Cumming, was travelling in China. The daughter of a wealthy landowner in Moray, Cumming had sufficient contacts, and resources, to allow her to travel widely. When she first came to Shanghai from

126 Liddell, *op. cit.* 78.
127 Liddell, *op. cit.*, 40.

Korea in 1878, she had already travelled in Australasia and the Pacific islands. After Shanghai, she visited Hong Kong and then made her way along the China coast calling at Guangzhou, and other treaty ports, before heading for Beijing. Cumming has often been criticised as being the prototype tourist, spending much of her time sightseeing and visiting her well–heeled contacts in China. Certainly, she makes little reference to the political tensions which existed between Chinese and western interests and perceptions.[128] However, when she was in Beijing in 1879 she, by chance, met a Scottish missionary, William Hill Murray, who had invented a system which allocated a number to different sounds in the Chinese language which allowed blind people to learn to read using Braille. She publicised his invention and, throughout her life, supported his efforts to help blind people in China.

Different images of China were created by another Scot, John Thompson, who was one of the first western photographers to travel throughout China where he recorded a wide variety of places, people and events, As a teenager, Thompson was apprenticed to an Edinburgh scientific instrument maker and attended evening classes at the Watt Institution and School of Arts. Like so many other ambitious young Scotsmen, Thompson's first venture abroad was to join a brother who was already working overseas, in this case in Singapore. He established a photographic studio there where, mostly, he took pictures of local European residents and their families. However, fascinated by the world beyond the confines of the Straits Settlements, he embarked on a series of photographic journeys to the Malaysian mainland, Sumatra, Sri Lanka and India, and then on to Thailand, Laos and Cambodia where he photographed the ruins at Angkor Wat. Returning to Britain in 1866, he was elected a Fellow of the Royal Geographical Society.

But the East still beckoned and, in the following year, he sailed again for Singapore, eventually settling in Hong Kong in 1868. Over the next five years, often only accompanied by his dog Spot, he travelled throughout China, creating a unique photographic record, not just of the cities and towns along the coast, but of the inland provinces of Hubei and Sichuan.

---

128 Kuehn, J., *Encounters with Otherness; Female Travellers in China, 1880-1929* in Kerr, D. and Kuehn, J., (Eds.), *A Century of Travels in China*, Hong Kong, Hong Kong University Press, 2007, 82-83.

His works on China included *Foochow and the River Min* (1873) and *Illustrations of China and its People,* (1873– 74).

The scope and diversity of Thompson's China photography was exceptional. It ranged from members of the imperial family, such as Prince Gong, to flower sellers and night watchmen. Thomson looked at China, not just with curious eyes, but with sympathetic insight. His pictures of a mother with her two children, or an old man with his mule, catch something of the poise and dignity of Chinese people. His photograph of the ruins of the sculptured terrace on Longevity Hill in Beijing demonstrates the wanton barbarity of the sacking of the Summer Palace in 1860.

He clearly interacted with the people he photographed, winning their confidence so that the pose was as natural as possible. His work and travels were facilitated by a wide range of local contacts, including missionaries, businessmen and government officials. Many of his more important contacts were Scots. The missionary, and scholar, Dr. John Dudgeon, helped him get around Beijing and organized his visit to the Summer Palace. When visiting Taiwan, he was accompanied by Dr. James Laidlaw Maxwell, who ran a medical mission in present day Kaohsiung for the Presbyterian Church of England. Both of them shared Thompson's passion for photography.

Whilst travellers like Bishop and Liddell wrote about their experiences of, and reactions to, China for an appreciative audience in the west, there were others who saw themselves, not as mere travellers, but as pioneers trying to identify economic and commercial opportunities for British capital and investors. A good example would be the larger-than-life, champagne loving, Archibald Ross Colquhoun, the fifth son of Dr Archibald Ross from Edinburgh who served in the EIC's Medical Service.

Colquhoun was educated at the Glasgow Academy and Helensburgh School and, later, at the Moravian Fathers School at Neuwied on the Rhine. He went to India in 1879 as an assistant surveyor with the Public Works Department. In a dazzling career as explorer, administrator and author, he travelled in 1881-82 between Guangzhou and Bhamo in Kachin State to survey a route for a possible railway along the old caravan route from China to Myanmar. (By a strange co-incidence, his guide for part of that journey was Gu Hongming who was a graduate of Edinburgh University). Colquhoun was *The Times* correspondent during the 1883 Franco-Chinese War and later, in 1894, became the Hongkong Bank's agent in Beijing. He had earlier been Deputy Commissioner in Upper Burma and the first Administrator of Mashonaland in southern Africa. Throughout his life, he travelled extensively also visiting Japan, the Philippines, the Dutch East Indies and North and South America.

Writing at the high-tide of Empire, Colquhoun's main works on China, *Across Chryse* (1883) and *Overland to China* (1900), highlight his view that China was ripe for investment and that if the British did not seize the opportunities arising, they would be outflanked by the other foreign powers in the region, particularly France and Russia. He believed the British needed to put aside "fickle democracy" and start to look after their own interests. "Great Britain has obtained from the Chinese government in the form of treaty rights and of concessions to British subjects, a number of legal or legitimate bases for claims in China," he wrote. "They are legal claims against all the world, but in order to be effective must be made good by action – perhaps by force."[129]

When Colquhoun travelled from Russia to China in 1898, again to determine the feasibility of constructing a railway line, he made his way from Lake Baikal, then the temporary terminus of the soon to be completed Trans-Siberian Railway, to Kyakhta on the southern Russian frontier. From there, he crossed the Mongolian steppes to Ulan Bator (Urga) and then on to Zhangjiakou (Kalgan) in Hebei Province close to Beijing The journey was, he remarked, tedious but "yet there is a certain charm about it, mainly, no doubt, the charm of novelty."[130]

As he travelled through the desert by camel and cart, he would have been aware that other Scots before him, like John Bell, had also made that journey. Indeed, he may have known that another fellow countryman, James Gilmore from Glasgow, had been travelling more recently in Mongolia and read his pioneering travelogue *Among the Monguls* which was first published in 1883.

---

129 Colquhoun, A. R., *Overland to China*, London, Harper & Brothers, 1900, 451-2.
130 Colquhoun, *op. cit.,* 258-59.

Gilmore was a robust, Protestant Christian who worked for the LMS in Mongolia from 1870 until his death from typhoid in 1891. Mongolia was seen as a very hard and lonely posting which it proved to be. Unusually for a missionary, Gilmore never made any converts in Mongolia but that was not for the want of trying. Right from the start, he travelled enormous distances in an effort to reach out to the people whom he met in the vast, sparsely populated hinterland and tried to learn their language. His first journey, which lasted fifteen months, took him from Beijing to Siberia and back. During this trip he visited Kyakhta, crossed Lake Baikal and stayed in Irkutsk where he saw the beautiful Epiphany Cathedral. Married in 1874, his wife, and later young family, accompanied him on journeys that took him all over Mongolia.

The pattern which gradually evolved in his life was to winter in Beijing, and spend the rest of the year travelling in Mongolia. Even if he was unsuccessful in making converts, he became a well-known figure. Returning once to Zhangjiakou, he was welcomed by a lama who, seeing him approach from a distance, ran round all the nearby tents shouting "He's come, He's come."[131]

Not surprisingly, over the years, he became despondent about whether it was worthwhile continuing missionary work in Mongolia. An independent and outspoken man, he fell out with colleagues, and suffered from the death of his wife in 1885 and then that of his youngest son two years later. Although he was in poor mental and physical health by the time he left Mongolia in 1889, for what was only his second holiday in twenty years, his legacy was readily assured. His courage and dedication were acknowledged after his death when he became known, simply, as the Apostle to the Mongols, taking on, in the eyes of the LMS and others, the heroic mantle of another Scot, David Livingstone. Reputations fade with time but Gilmore's writings, particularly *Among the Mongols*, provide a unique and sensitive anthropological insight into a society about which little was known, or understood, at that time.

---

131 Lodwick, K. L., *The Legacy of James Gilmour* in *International Bulletin of Missionary Research*, Jan 2003, Vol. 27, Issue 1, 35.

Wherever they came from, all travellers to China, and beyond, were conscious they were engaging with societies very different from their own. Some came with preconceived notions about the value of western ideas and institutions; others were more open minded in their approach to China and its people. Although they would have debated amongst themselves the nature of their responses, there is little doubt their travel experiences changed them by opening up wider vistas of other people, places and ideas which differentiated them from their contacts at home in Europe or elsewhere.

All of them wrote and talked, often passionately, about what they had seen, what they had heard and what they had learnt. So we find travellers, like Isabella Bird Bishop, addressing the Royal Geographical Society and complaining she was always on the move to talk to groups around Britain. James Gilmore addressed missionary and religious groups about his experiences as well. One can see a packed hall of soberly dressed people waiting patiently to hear him speak. The society in which *they* lived - the rumbling tramcars outside, the faint smell of rose water and moth balls - was all so very different from the life, and people, he had known. As the last echoes of the opening hymn quietly faded, and Gilmore rose to speak, perhaps his mind flashed back to *his* world - the distant Great Wall, the circle of yurts, the brightly dressed lamas, the smell of boiling mutton, the ever piercing winter cold, camel bells in the lonely desert and the wide, and cloudless, Mongolian sky.

8 Beyond another Wall – the Chinese in Scotland

Chinese people don't see things differently, we see different things from the same vantage point.

JIANG YI.

The first recorded visit of a Chinese person to Britain was Shen Fuzong, a Jesuit scholar, who met James 11 (James V11 of Scotland) in 1686 in London. James was so impressed by Shen that he asked him to sit for Godfrey Kneller, the leading portrait artist of his day. His painting *The Chinese Convert* was hung in the King's bedchamber. Sadly, Shen did not make it back to China - he died on his way home.

It is not known who was the first Chinese to visit Scotland – possibly a sailor on a vessel plying between China and Britain in the early nineteenth century as trade started to expand or, perhaps, an itinerant peddler who had made his way from northern China, through Siberia and across mainland Europe to Scotland's east coast. As noted earlier, Chinese students came to Scotland in the nineteenth century, one of the first being Huang Kuan who graduated with an MD from Edinburgh University in 1855. But from the 1860s onwards, there were also other visitors who provide an interesting insight into Scottish society and their perceptions of it.

Wang Tao was one of the best informed, and well known, scholars of nineteenth century China. Born in 1828 near Suzhou in Jiangsu Province in eastern China, he came to Shanghai in 1849 where he was employed as a translator with the LMS printing press. After being associated with the Taiping revolutionaries, he had to flee to Hong Kong where he was introduced to James Legge, then in the process of translating the Chinese canonical texts. The two men worked together for ten years and became firm friends.

After Legge returned to Europe on leave in 1867, Wang joined him, spending much of his time at Legge's home in Dollar, where they completed the translation of *The Book of Songs*, *I Ching* and *The Book of Rites*. In his leisure time, Wang enjoyed roaming in the surrounding countryside, and over the Ochil hills, but he also visited other parts of Scotland. When in Edinburgh, he visited the University where he was impressed to find students studying what he called "practical" subjects such as astronomy, mathematics, geography and foreign languages.

As with the delegation from Meiji Japan, led by Tomomi Iwakura, which visited Britain in 1872, Wang was interested in new industrial developments and processes. In Edinburgh, he visited a mechanised printing works; in Aberdeen's granite quarries, the massive grinding and polishing equipment captured his attention; in Dundee, he visited a textile mill which employed over two thousand workers. He later wrote about his time in Europe in *Jottings of Carefree Travel*, one of the earliest pieces of modern travel writing about the west by a Chinese intellectual.[132]

Wang's frequent association with foreigners in China, and his visit to Europe, gave him an appreciation of western philosophy and scholarship which few other Chinese thinkers of his generation possessed. From this understanding, he began to develop new insights into the constraints, and challenges, facing Chinese society which he published in his newspaper *Tsun–wan yat-po* established in Hong Kong in 1874. His insightful articles and editorials have led Wang to be regarded as the first political columnist of modern China.[133]

---

132 Cohen, P. A., *Between Tradition and Modernity; Wang Tao and Reform in Late Ching China*, Cambridge, Massachusetts, Harvard University Press, 1988, 70-71.
133 Xiantao Zhang, *The Origins of the Modern Chinese Press; the influence of the Protestant missionary press in late Qing China*, Abingdon, Routledge, 2007, 64.

Shortly before his death in 1897, Wang was visited by an up and coming young patriot, Sun Zhongshan (Sun Yat-sen), fresh from his medical training under James Cantlie at the College of Medicine for Chinese in Hong Kong. Wang and Sun probably discussed politics, and the need for reform in China, but perhaps also, in a moment of reflection, they may have remembered the two men from faraway Scotland who had influenced each of them in different ways and whose thinking encouraged them in their search for a new China.

Another visitor was Jiang Yi who, disillusioned with the politics and violence of the time, came to study in Britain in 1933. Jiang was a scholar and administrator who, during his twenty two year stay in Britain, penned a series of travel books about the places he visited. All of them were entitled *The Silent Traveller in …* locations as diverse as London, the Lake District and Oxford. Published in 1948, *The Silent Traveller in Edinburgh* provides an evocative, often whimsical, perspective of Edinburgh, and Scotland, from the viewpoint of a Chinese visitor during the Second World War.

Jiang first came to Edinburgh in 1937, and revisited the city again in 1943, and 1944. He was captivated by the cityscape as well as by the surrounding hills and the adjacent sea. "Chinese people don't see things differently," he once explained, "we see different things from the same vantage point."[134] Looking at the Lion's Haunch on Arthur's Seat he saw, not a lion, but an elephant nestling in the hollow! He thought the scenery in Scotland very similar to that of China and suggested that was why the Chinese and the Scots "have so much in common in their human nature." He also came to believe that the Chinese and the Scots shared a sense of the comparative value of things and understood the virtue of being thrifty.

In what he remembered was often "drizzling rain" he visited all the major tourist sites including the Castle, the Closes off the Royal Mile, the Braid Hills, the beach at Portobello and the Zoo. As he tried to understand the historical background, he often interpreted what he saw in the context of Chinese history and literature. Moreover, he had a keen eye for the people he met on his travels and their response to him. Walking one rainy Sunday

---

134 Yee, C., *The Silent Traveller in Edinburgh,* London, Methuen, 1948, 19, 23, 26, 52, 56, 95, 103, 129.

morning through the Meadows, he noted that most churchgoers were either elderly or very young – and almost all carried a Bible. He regretted that many of the books written about China by missionaries portrayed his fellow countrymen as superstitious fatalists. Would it not be better, he thought, to seek parallels between Christianity and Confucianism rather than differences? Coming across some Chinese language books in the University Library, he was saddened to learn that they were seldom used. He wondered why people in Scotland didn't spend as much time learning Chinese as the Chinese spent learning English.

Standing outside John Knox's house, he was surrounded by a group of smiling children clearly wondering what he was doing there. "Chinee" they shouted and laughed – as did he. Going down to the Canongate he went into a small pub, one of about twenty in the area. There were only three customers, an old man and two even more elderly women wrapped in black shawls, who were in animated conversation with the barman. When Jiang entered, silence descended; they looked at him with a mixture of curiosity and hostility. He drank his beer in silence. It's a long way from Nanjing to the Canongate!

Other people he encountered were less reserved. Walking past the Tron Kirk one Sunday evening a passer-by, whose breath was "strong enough to overpower the evening mist", tapped him on the shoulder and launched into Shanghai Pidgin English. "Come with me. We have drink together. I am citizen of the world. I am a Glasgow man. All Glasgow men go round the world. I went to your country when I was a sailor. Edinburgh pub - no go, no go!" Pointing to the two bottles in his overcoat pockets, he urged Jiang to come with him for a "better drink". Jiang graciously declined. "No drinky"! Perhaps it was a fitting end to his visit to Edinburgh!

When Jiang visited Scotland, the Chinese population there was tiny. The 1931 Census had shown that the China born population was seven hundred and sixty. As this number included people of non-Chinese ethnic origin, such as Europeans born in China, and excluded ethnic Chinese from British colonies, the actual number of Chinese in Scotland was probably less than stated.[135] The story of Chinese engagement with

---

135 From the 1991 Census to date, the ethnic origin of those enumerated is recorded allowing a more detailed assessment to be made of Chinese demographics in Britain.

Scottish, indeed British, society has often been characterised as "salt, soap and soy" representing, in sequence, the main employment focus of many Chinese immigrants as sailors, laundry operators and restaurant workers.

The switch from sail to steam in the middle years of the nineteenth century provided employment opportunities for sailors, first from India, and then from China, on the trunk shipping routes, the so called arteries of empire, that were developing between Britain and her far flung possessions and areas of influence overseas. Since the late eighteenth century, the EIC had employed Indian seamen to make up the shortfall of British sailors conscripted into the Royal Navy during time of war. They were also employed because of the high sickness, and death, rates experienced by European sailors in warm climates. Poverty and political instability, no doubt, encouraged Chinese seafarers to seek employment with the major British lines. Whether Indian or Chinese, they were lumped together as "lascars" - from the Bengali for sailor or militiaman. Although they came from different ethnic backgrounds, they shared one thing in common – they were cheap in comparison with their European counterparts.

In the early years of the twentieth century Indian and Chinese deckhands were being paid about a quarter of what European sailors earned. They were therefore an important component of the seagoing workforce for companies like the Scottish controlled Clan Line, and other major operators such as P&O and the Blue Funnel Line.[136] Although the number of Chinese sailors visiting Glasgow increased from one thousand, two hundred and forty three in 1904 to three thousand, two hundred and fifty three in 1913, they were never more than three per cent of the total crew on British registered ships calling at that port. The majority worked as firemen in the engine room, stoking the boilers, as this job was unpopular with Europeans because of the high temperatures experienced, particularly in the tropics. As well as being financially disadvantaged, Indian and Chinese sailors were also entitled to less space (2.1 cu. meters against 3.4 cu. meters for a European), and there were regular complaints about the quality of food available at sea.

---

136 Visram, R., *Asians in Britain; 400 Years of History*, London and Sterling, V A, Pluto Press, 2002, 54-55

Indian and Chinese sailors first came to ports like London and Liverpool, rather than Glasgow, because of the logistical problems of deepening the Clyde to allow large seagoing vessels close to the heart of the city. Work on improving the river had been in progress since 1768 when John Golborne suggested that rubble jetties be constructed to enhance the flow, but it was not until the Clyde Navigation Trust was set up nearly a century later that significant progress was made with the provision of over twenty thousand square meters of water space at the Kingston Dock in 1867. Queens Dock followed in 1880, Princes Dock in 1900 and Rothesay Dock at Clydebank in 1907. By that date, Glasgow was the third largest port in the UK in terms of net registry after London and Liverpool.

When they arrived in Glasgow, Indian and Chinese sailors would have faced racial exclusion and hostility. Following the Boxer rising, the early years of the twentieth century echoed with concerns about the "yellow peril" with people of Chinese origin being demonised as sub-human. Workers objected to "coolie labour" which they saw as threatening the jobs, not just of sailors, but miners and other lower paid workers as well. During the national seamen's strike of 1911, Indian and Chinese sailors were vilified as unprofessional – the National Sailors' and Firemen's Union even suggesting that "in times of emergency inexperienced or coloured seamen are unfit to rise to the emergency and thereby the safety of those aboard is compromised".[137] In such circumstances, it is not surprising that few chose to jump ship in Scotland and there is little evidence that many did. However, if the pattern at London and Liverpool was repeated, there may have been a few who did so, possibly marrying local, or Irish, girls and setting up small eateries, laundries or boarding houses in the dock area.

Agitation against the employment of Indian and Chinese sailors subsided during the First World War when many of them served in the British merchant fleet because their white counterparts had been called up to the Royal Navy. In the economic dislocation immediately after the end of the war, hostility to the employment of "coloured seamen" was quick to surface. At the Glasgow Mercantile Marine Office in 1921

---

137 McFarland, E. W., *Clyde opinion on an old controversy: Indian and Chinese seafarers in Glasgow* in *Ethnic and Racial Studies*, Vol. 14, No. 4, 1991, 506-07

a demonstration against the employment of "Asiatics" turned violent and a number of sailors, and others, were injured. During the Second World War some twenty thousand Chinese were recruited by the Royal Navy to help keep Britain's western approaches open during the Battle of the Atlantic. After the war most were repatriated quickly to China. The Chinese community that remained in Scotland was tiny but it was to be topped up by the fresh migration of people from Hong Kong.

In the wake of the 1949 revolution in China thousands of people fled to Hong Kong, many directly across the border from neighbouring Guangdung Province. Within a short period of time, Hong Kong's population had quadrupled, placing an enormous strain on government services. Many of the newcomers squatted on land in the New Territories, in parts of urban Kowloon, and on Hong Kong Island.[138] At the same time, the Hong Kong Government started importing cheap rice and encouraged small farmers to grow vegetables so as to avoid being dependent on China for supplies. Traditional agriculture was quickly undermined and, with a tight job market elsewhere in Hong Kong, poorer farmers started to look to other opportunities overseas.[139]

The small core of established Chinese restaurants, mainly in London and the south-east of England, provided a start for many villagers from the New Territories. But they quickly broke away to open their own restaurants to take advantage of the growing trend in the fifties of going out to eat and trying more exotic types of cuisine. The first Chinese restaurant in Glasgow was reputedly the *Wah Yen* at 455 Govan Road, opened by Jimmy Yih in the late 1940s. Opened about the same time, *Ping On* in Deanhaugh Street is supposed to be the oldest Chinese restaurant in Edinburgh.

The Chinese community in Scotland grew steadily although it was not evenly dispersed across the country. In 1981, using information from the electoral role, the Scottish Office estimated that almost two-thirds of the Chinese population of Scotland was urban based, with sixty five

---

138 Welsh, F., *A History of Hong Kong*, London, Harper Collins, 1993, 444; Hayes, J., *Friends and Teachers*, Hong Kong, Hong Kong University Press, 1996, 7.
139 Benton, G and Gomez, E. T., *The Chinese in Britain, 1800 - Present*, London, Palgrave Macmillan, 2011, 36.

per cent located in Strathclyde and Lothian.[140] The 1991 Census showed a total ethnic Chinese population in Scotland of ten thousand, four hundred and seventy six of whom one thousand, nine hundred and forty were in Edinburgh, two thousand, seven hundred and eighty in Glasgow and seven hundred and eight in Aberdeen. The census of 2001 showed the ethnic Chinese population of Scotland had increased by some fifty five per cent to sixteen thousand, three hundred and ten making the Chinese the third largest ethnic group in Scotland after Pakistanis and Indians.

The data provided in the 2001 census about place of birth points to the changing composition, and diversity, of the ethnic Chinese community in Scotland which, immediately after 1945, drew most of its immigrants from the New Territories of Hong Kong. The 2001 data shows that some forty five per cent were born in the "Far East" (excluding China), whilst just under thirty per cent were born in Scotland and eighteen per cent in China itself. Many of those born in the "Far East" and China would have come to Scotland for secondary or tertiary education, as economic migrants, or as asylum seekers. The 2001 census data also confirms that catering and associated distribution, retail and wholesale undertakings continue as the main form of employment for Chinese people in Scotland. Other areas of employment include health, property and social work.[141]

In considering the history and development of the Chinese community in Scotland it is important to bear in mind that, as of 2001, it represented only 0.3 per cent of Scotland's population. For many post-1945 Chinese immigrants, the principal objective was to get a job, stay alive and provide as best they could for their families in Scotland, or elsewhere in Hong Kong, or China. Of those early immigrants, very few spoke English with any degree of proficiency. As with earlier immigrants to Scotland, like the Irish, the Italians, Jews and Lithuanians, it was to their fellow countrymen that they looked for friendship and support. Moreover, be-

---

140 Bailey, N., Bowes, A and Sim, D., *The Chinese Community in Scotland* in *Scottish Geographical Magazine*, 110; 2, 1994, 67 - 8.

141 Bell, E. M., *An anthropological study of ethnicity and the reproduction of culture among Hong Kong Chinese families in Scotland*, London School of Economics and Political Science, unpublished PhD thesis. 2011.

cause of actual, or threatened, racial abuse, which was never far from the takeaway door, the Chinese community in Scotland, as elsewhere in Britain and Ireland, tended to be self-effacing and reluctant to engage with mainstream society.

This situation began to change from the early 1970s as immigrants, and more particularly their families, started to put down roots in Scotland. With the New Territories being urbanized at a frenetic rate, and clouds hanging over the political future of Hong Kong, the idea of returning home to build a new house in a rural village surrounded by high rise housing certainly became less attractive. Additionally, as more and more takeaways were set up in Scotland, there was a real possibility of making good money, even if the work was hard and the hours long for all the family.

Chinese community identity began to be more fully expressed with the setting up of "Chinese" schools in different parts of urban Scotland. In part, this was in response to the demise of the grandparent generation, and recognition that, if home was to be Scotland, it would be necessary to nurture Chinese culture and ideas in the coming generations.[142] Local Authority support for minority ethnic groups, and the growth in interest in all things related to an emergent China, facilitated this process. A Chinese school was established in Edinburgh in 1971 and one in Glasgow in 1972. A Chinese school followed in Aberdeen in 1991 and a second one in Edinburgh in 1994. Their aim was to promote Chinese culture and the teaching of Chinese. However, these schools did not operate normally as independent, full time entities but as adjuncts to existing educational facilities, such as Stow College in Glasgow, where evening and weekend courses were offered. The schools were located adjacent to areas where Chinese people had settled in the cities, such as the Garnethill area in Glasgow, and the Marchmont district of Edinburgh. Today, these schools serve as a focus for other community activities, including celebration of the Lunar New Year, art classes etc. In parallel, community organisations were set up focusing on the welfare needs of the Chinese community. Examples would be the Chinese Community Development Partnership in Glasgow, and the Chinese Elderly Support Association in Edinburgh. On cultural matters, the Ricefield Arts Centre

---

142 Benton and Gomez, *op cit.*, 188 - 89.

in Glasgow, established in 2004, aims to promote, and advance, Chinese arts and crafts in Scotland.

Chinese material culture in Scotland is well represented through the collection of bronzes, ceramics, furniture and jades in the Burrell collection in Glasgow. An entrepreneur and ship owner, William Burrell never visited China – but he had a keen eye for items of beauty and value from around the world, as well as from the past. The reason for Burrell's interest in Chinese ceramics is unclear but he put together a collection which covers over five thousand years of China's long ceramic history.[143]

Although there were traditional Chinatowns in London, Liverpool and Cardiff, dating back to when Chinese people first came to Britain, they were slow to develop in Scotland, largely because of the small size of the ethnic Chinese population, and their wide dispersal around the country. A small Chinatown was opened in the Cowcaddens in Glasgow in 1998 and provides a range of retail and wholesale outlets as well as large restaurants. But the scale of operations was small. An analysis in 2008 of companies in the UK owned by British Chinese showed that only five out of one hundred and fourteen were based in Scotland.[144]

Religion has always played an important part in the life of Chinese people whether that is ancestor worship, Confucianism or Christianity - and the Chinese community in Scotland is no exception. Even if sometimes strained by the spirit of enquiry implicit in western style education, filial respect is expected, and lauded, in all Chinese communities. There are Chinese Christian churches in Aberdeen, Glasgow and Edinburgh. All are evangelical in theology and hold services in Chinese and/or English.

Christian meeting places for Chinese people are not, of course, restricted to the main cities but have emerged in other areas where Chinese migrants settled such as Dundee where there is an active Chinese Christian Fellowship. The True Jesus Church of Elgin, a small town of some twenty five thousand, in Morayshire, north east Scotland, provides an interesting example of Chinese migrants maintaining their cultural and religious identity and witnessing to their beliefs in a foreign

---

143 Glasgow Museums, *The Burrell Collection,* Glasgow, Harper-Collins, New Edition 1997, 42.

144 Benton and Gomez, *op. cit.* 370 -78.

community. The True Jesus Church in Elgin traces its beginnings to the early Pentecostal movement in China in the 1920's. Most of the members of the Elgin Church came from Ap Chau (Duck Island) just off the Kowloon peninsula in Hong Kong. They went to the Elgin area in pursuit of opportunities in the catering trade and established, first, a prayer house in 1977 and then a Church in 1981.[145] The Church became, not just a place for religious worship, but a community centre as well in which all parts of the Elgin Chinese community play a role.

One of the more enduring areas of engagement between Scotland and China has been the Scotland-China Association (SCA) established in 1966. The Association emerged from the break-up of the Britain-China Friendship Association in the wake of the Sino-Soviet split in the early 1960s. The aim of the SCA is to foster friendship and understanding between the people of Scotland and China.

The Association's first Chairman was the Rev. T. Ralph Morton, one time deputy leader of the Iona Community, who had worked as a missionary for the United Free Church of Scotland, and the Church of Scotland, in Shenyang and elsewhere in northern China between 1925 and 1937. The Vice Chairmen were the sinologist John Chinnery who, in the previous year, had been appointed as the first head of the new Chinese Department at Edinburgh University and the historian, John Gray, from Glasgow University. Still an active member of the Association, Elsie Collier was its first Secretary. The Association lined up an impressive list of supporters including Lord Boyd Orr, the Nobel Peace Prize winner, the Chairman of the Scottish Land Court, Lord Birsay, the author Compton Mackenzie, the educationalist Dr. H. Stewart Mackintosh, Norman W. Porteous, Principal of New College, Edinburgh and Bruno Schotz, the sculptor and a member of the Royal Scottish Academy. Tam Dalyell, one time Father of the House of Commons, became a Vice-President in 1972, a post he continues to hold today.

Although the early focus of the Association was on education, it embraced a range of activities, working closely with the Scottish universities to provide information about China including artistic events, film

---

145 Liu, G., *The Role of the True Jesus Church in the Communal Development of the Chinese People in Elgin, Scotland* in Sinn, E., (Ed.),*The Last Half Century of Chinese Overseas*, Hong Kong, Hong Kong University Press, 1998, 425-446.

shows about China and concerts by visiting Chinese musicians. As trade with China expanded, the Association started a China Business Club with a view to facilitating contacts amongst people from Scotland who were doing business in China. The Association also works with visiting Chinese students and scholars in Scotland, welcoming them to its meetings. Although the Association has never had more than a few hundred members, its influence has been significant, particularly at a time when there is growing public interest in China. With a membership that reflects all sections of Scottish society, the Association has survived, and flourishes, largely because it maintains its focus on promoting Sino-Scottish friendship – and not being unduly concerned with political arguments![146]

Wang Tao would have marvelled both at the existence of the SCA and at how far the Chinese community in Scotland has come since he first visited nearly a hundred and fifty years ago. Like all immigrant groups, the Chinese community has faced exclusion and prejudice but has survived, changed, and grown to become a significant ethnic group in Scotland, proud of its strong traditions, and confident about its future role in a changing Scotland. To paraphrase Mao Zedong's famous remarks in September 1949, the Chinese people have stood up not only in China but in Scotland as well.

---

146 A detailed history of the Scotland-China Association is given in the articles by John Chinnery and Elsie Collier in the Spring 2006 edition of *Sine,* the Journal of the Scotland-China Association.

9 Scotland and China – a new journey?

He who takes the longest strides, does not walk the fastest.

LAO TZU.

We have explored why people from Scotland, one of the smallest, remotest countries in Europe, came to have such an influence on one of the largest nations in the world, China, in the nineteenth and twentieth centuries. In this context, the themes running through this period are aggressive, commercially driven, western intervention in China, and attempts to change Chinese lifestyles, modes of belief and ways of thinking. In parallel, struggling initially but eventually triumphant, we have seen also how Chinese nationalist sentiment was, first, to oust the Qing dynasty and, eventually after invasion and war, to destroy the labyrinth of influential foreign business, educational and social networks which inhibited the development of Chinese identity. As Mao Zedong remarked in 1949 "Ours will no longer be a nation subject to insult and humiliation. We have stood up."[147]

Sixty years after the last Scots left new China what is the status of Sino-Scottish relations? Will Scotland and China have something to share in the future on economic, social or, indeed, political issues?

---

147 Mao Zedong, *Opening Address*, First Plenary Session of the Chinese People's Political Consultative Conference, 21 September 1949.

They certainly have much to build on. Scots made an important contribution to the development of medicine in China as well as the establishment of educational institutions at all levels. They also helped extend trade and commerce, as well as banking and finance; they played an important role in the growth of China's economic infrastructure, including railways and shipping. They influenced Chinese people to examine the demands of Christianity – many Chinese Christians today trace their faith back to these early pioneers.

There were downsides too of Scottish influence in China. As well as overbearing aggressive traders, who cared for little other than profit, there was the scourge of the narcotics trade both on those who perpetrated it and those who were abused by it. Certainly, Scots could be as racist and abusive as others with little sensitivity to people trying to make sense of a different world view, and ways of thinking and behaving.

Nevertheless, although the Scots always had a very fine view of themselves as Scots wherever they went, including China, one can detect often something of a Scottish empathy for the people they encountered abroad and the circumstances in which they found themselves. David Livingstone said he understood Africans better than others because they lived in a clan system like many people in Scotland. Fifty years later Andrew Dewar Gibb repeated a now familiar refrain. The Scot is "a hard worker and less interested than the Englishman in the artificial distinctions between classes. He is more democratic and less insular."[148]

Although their views were probably overstated in both cases, they do point to a Scottish willingness to appreciate the viewpoint of people from different cultures and backgrounds. Derived from the thinking of the Scottish Enlightenment, and a strong democratic religious tradition, Scots in China, and elsewhere, were perhaps more disposed to reach out over a chasm of "otherness" to try and understand the individual in his personal, societal and historic context. We have come across many examples of people who tried to respond to China, and its people, not for how they were supposed to be perceived, but for what they really were. Writing about the Chinese, Dugald Christie was emphatic about their qualities. "Their family affection, their staunch friendship, their unselfishness to those they love, their homely joys, their love of children, their

---

148 Gibb, A. D., *Scottish Empire*, London, Alexander MacLehose, 1937, 308-09.

kindliness to friends and neighbours, their warm-hearted gratitude, their fortitude in trouble, their patience in enduring, will compare with those of any nation."

However, that understanding was often less apparent in Scotland than in China. Over the years, new ethnic and religious minorities in Scotland faced opposition, exclusion and abuse – and the Chinese were no exception. As the fledgling Chinese community expanded in Scotland, it remained essentially inward looking, drawing on such support as was available from other immigrants from China and Chinese communities overseas. Nevertheless, although the process of assimilation into Scottish society was to be a slow one, it was hastened by events, not in Scotland, but in China.

As the Maoist era came to an end in the late 1970s, China began again to engage, at first tentatively, but then more confidently, with the wider world beyond its borders which had been closed effectively since 1949. Mao, who had died in September 1976, left his successors daunting challenges, the most pressing of which was how to fuel economic growth and agricultural productivity to meet the basic needs of a rapidly expanding population. The Great Leap Forward, and the Cultural Revolution, had been disasters which left China isolated and technologically backward.

A survivor of the Long March, and the Cultural Revolution, Deng Xiaoping was the man who would make China a dynamic economic powerhouse and, within forty years, one of the world's leading economies. If the economy of China was to be modernised, Deng realised, China needed access to foreign investment, management and, most importantly, technology. Initially, through Special Economic Zones, such as that of Shenzhen on the Hong Kong border, and then across much of the country, modernisation of China's economy took off at a frenetic rate. The race to catch up became a national obsession.

Although the major focus of China's trade was with the US, Japan and the major European economies, a range of Scottish businesses entered the China market, usually on a joint venture basis, where they had skills, or products, relevant to China's modernisation programmes. Examples would be major companies such as the Weir Group and Clyde Blowers as well as more diverse operations ranging from Whyte and Mackay, the distillers, to Martin Currie Investment Management. Today, over forty Scottish companies are active in China. Much Scottish investment in China is facilitated by Scottish Development International which operates representative offices in Beijing, Shanghai and Hong Kong. The current focus is on promoting investment in growth industries like food and drink, energy, business services, technology, and life sciences in which Scotland has recognised strengths.

The speed and scope of China's modernisation prompted the Scottish Executive in August 2006 to develop a China strategy to strengthen Scotland's engagement with China "for the mutual benefit of both our nations."[149] Acknowledging China's growing "economic cultural and political importance", the strategy envisaged that Scotland position itself so as to take full advantage of the trading, and other opportunities, emerging in China. From raising understanding of Chinese language and culture in Scotland to expanding tourism and educational connections, a ten-point plan was formulated, focusing initially on projects in Beijing, Guangdung and Shandong Provinces, Shanghai and Hong Kong.

The China strategy was reaffirmed and updated in May 2008 with the emphasis being on building on past achievements and developing representation of Scotland in China that was independent of wider UK programmes. Scotland was to be promoted as a distinctive global identity.[150] In December 2011, Scotland's First Minister, Alex Salmond, led a delegation to China where he met Vice Minister Chen Jian at the Ministry of Commerce in Beijing. They agreed to establish a bilateral high-level forum to facilitate Scottish and Chinese company introductions, with meetings to be held alternatively in China and Scotland.

Since the 1980's a variety of cultural, educational and scientific links have developed between Scotland and China, often building on those pioneered by the Scotland-China Association. Chinese people are proud of being the world's oldest continuous civilization and are happy to share their cultural heritage with people around the world. Scotland has hosted

---

149 Scottish Executive, *Scotland's strategy for stronger engagement with China*, August 2006.

150 Scottish Government, *The Scottish Government's Refreshed China Plan*, May 2008.

exhibitions of Chinese art and ceramics as well as circus, dance and opera performances. As noted earlier, Scotland's universities have entered into a number of joint venture agreements with tertiary institutions in China. Such agreements are likely to increase in the future, particularly where Scottish expertise, and knowhow, is valued as a contribution to China's modernisation. In 2005 the Royal Society of Edinburgh signed a Memorandum of Understanding with the Chinese Academy of Sciences to encourage collaboration on scientific research and exchange programmes between Scotland and China. More importantly for most people in Scotland, two Giant Pandas, Tian Tian (Sweetie) and Yang Guang (Sunshine) arrived in Edinburgh Zoo from China in December 2011.They have probably done more to stimulate interest in China than many other initiatives!

With or without Giant Pandas, Scottish interaction with emerging China is at an early stage. It is difficult to predict its outcome. However, in whatever way that relationship evolves, it will be defined by many shared past associations, connections and memories. Taken together, they are a significant dynamic in the modern history of two very diverse nations at opposite ends of the world.

Select Bibliography

Airlie, S., *Thistle and Bamboo*, Hong Kong, Oxford University Press, 1989.

Bailey, P. J., *Reform the People; Changing Attitudes towards Popular Education in Early Twentieth-Century China,* Edinburgh, Edinburgh University Press, 1990.

Balme, H., *China and Modern Medicine,* London, Church Missionary Society, 1921.

Bell, E. M., *An anthropological study of ethnicity and the reproduction of culture among Hong Kong Chinese families in Scotland,* London School of Economics and Political Science, Unpublished PhD Thesis, 2011.

Bell, J., *Travels from St. Petersburg in Russia to various parts of Asia,* Edinburgh and Glasgow, W. Creech and R. & A. Foulis, 1788.

Benton, G., and Gomez, E. T., *The Chinese in Britain, 1800 – Present,* London, Palgrave, Macmillan, 2011.

Bishop, I. B., *The Yangtze Valley and Beyond,* London, John Murray, 1899.

Blyth, S., and Wotherspoon, I., *Hong Kong Remembers*, Hong Kong, Oxford University Press, 1996.

Brunero, D., *Britain's Imperial Cornerstone in China,* Abingdon, Routeledge, 2006.

Calder, J. M., *Scotland's March Past,* London, London Missionary Society, 1945.

Campbell, R. S., *James Duncan Campbell; A Memoir by his Son*, Cambridge, Massachusetts, Harvard University Press, 1970.

Casserly, G., *The Land of the Boxers; Or China Under the Allies*, London, Longmans & Green, 1903.

Cannon, I. D., *Public success, private sorrow; the life and times of Henry Brewitt-Taylor (1857-1938),* Hong Kong, Hong Kong University Press, 2009.

Choa, G. H., *The Life and Times of Sir Kai Ho Kai,* Hong Kong, Chinese University Press, 1981.

Chang, E. H., *Britain's Chinese Eye,* Stanford, Stanford University Press, 2010.

Christie, D., *Thirty Years in Moukden, 1883-1913*, London, Constable and Company, 1914.

Chow, Tse-tsung, *The May Fourth Movement,* Cambridge, Massachusetts and London, Harvard University Press, 1960.

Coates, P. D., *The China Consuls; British Consular Officers, 1843-1943*, Oxford, Oxford University Press, 1988.

Cohen, P. A., *Between Tradition and Modernity; Wang Tao and Reform in Late Ching China*, Cambridge, Massachusetts, Harvard University Press, 1988.

Colquhoun, A. R., *Overland to China,* London, Harper & Brothers, 1900.

Crichton-Browne, J., *The Life of Sir Halliday Macartney*, London, John Lane, 1908.

Dawin, D., *British Women Missionaries in Nineteenth Century China*, London, Taylor & Francis, 1992.

De Gruche, K., *Dr. D. Duncan Main of Hangchow*, London & Edinburgh, Marshall, Morgan & Scott, 1930.

Dupee, J. N., *British Travel Writers in China – Writing Home to a British Public*, 1890-1914, New York, The Edwin Mellon Press, c 2004.

Forrest, D., *Tea for the British*, London, Chatto & Windus, 1973.

Fortune, R., *Three Years Wanderings in the Northern Provinces of China*, London, John Murray, 1847; *A Journey to the Tea Countries of China*, London, John Murray, 1852.

Furth, C., *Ting Wen-chiang,* Cambridge, Massachusetts, Harvard University Press, 1970.

Gilbert, R., What's wrong with China, New York, Frederick A. Stokes, 1926.

Glasgow Museums, *The Burrell Collection,* Glasgow, Harper Collins, New Edition, 1997.

Gordon Cumming, C. F., *Wanderings in China,* Edinburgh, Blackwood, 1886.

Grypma, S., *Healing Henan; Canadian Nurses at the North China Mission,* Vancouver, University of British Columbia Press, Press, 2008.

Hancock, C., *Robert Morrison and the Birth of Chinese Protestantism,* London, T. & T. Clark, 2008.

Hargreaves, J. D., *Academe and Empire,* Aberdeen, Aberdeen University Press, 1994.

Hayes, J., *Friends and Teachers,* Hong Kong, Hong Kong University Press, 1996.

Hayhoe, R., *China's Universities, 1895-1995,* New York and London, Garland, 1996.

Haynes, D. M., *Imperial medicine; Patrick Manson and the conquest of tropical disease,* Philadelphia, University of Pennsylvania Press, 2001.

Hevia, J. L., *English Lessons; The Pedagogy of Imperialism in Nineteenth-Century China,* Durham NC, Duke University Press, 2003.

Huenemann, R. W., *The Dragon and the Iron Horse, the Economics of Railroads in China, 1876-1937,* Cambridge, Massachusetts and London, Harvard University Press, 1984.

Hume, D., *Essays; Moral Political and Literary,* Edinburgh, James Clarke, 1809.

James, A. T. S., *Twenty-Five Years of the LMS,* London, London Missionary Society, 1923.

Jones, S., *Two Centuries of Overseas Trading; the Origins and Growth of the Inchcape Group,* London, Macmillan, 1986.

Kerr, D., and Kuehn, J., (Eds.), *A Century of Travels in China*, Hong Kong, Hong Kong University Press, 2007.

Le Pichon, A., *China Trade and Empire,* Oxford, Oxford University Press, 2006.

Levine, M. A., *The Found Generation; Chinese Communists in Europe during the Twenties*, Seattle and London, University of Washington Press, 1993.

Lian Xi, *Redeemed by Fire - The Rise of Popular Christianity in Modern China,* New Haven and London, Yale University Press, 2010.

Lindsay, A., *Seeds of Blood and Beauty*, Edinburgh, Birlinn, 2005.

Liddell, T. H., *China, Its Marvel and Mystery*, New York, John Lane Company, 1910.

Lim, P., *Forgotten Souls; A Social History of the Hong Kong Cemetery*, Hong Kong, Hong Kong University Press, 2011.

Lo Hui-Min (Ed.), *The Correspondence of G. E. Morrison,* Cambridge, Cambridge University Press, 1978.

Lubbock, B., *The China Clippers*, Glasgow, James Brown & Son, 1914.

Lutz, J. G., *China and the Christian Colleges, 1850-1950*, Ithaca and London, Cornell University Press, 1971.

MacGregor, D. R., *The Tea Clippers*, London, Percival, Marshall & Co. Ltd., 1952.

Markham, C. R., *Narratives of the Mission of George Bogle to Tibet and of the Journey of Thomas Manning to Lhasa*, London, Trubner and Co., 1876.

McCasland, D., *Eric Liddell – Pure Gold*, Grand Rapids, Discovery House Publishers, 2001.

Morrison, E., *Memoirs of the Life and Labours of Robert Morrison,* London, Longman, Orme, Brown, Green, 1839.

Mui, H. C. and Mui, L. H., (Eds.), *William Melrose in China, 1845-1855,* Edinburgh, Scottish History Society, 1973.

Nicholson, M., and O'Neill, M., *Glasgow – Locomotive Builder to the World,* Edinburgh and Glasgow, Polygon, Third Eye Centre, Springburn Museum, 1987.

Platt, S., *Autumn in the Heavenly Kingdom*, London, Atlantic Books, 2012.

Preston, D., *The Boxer Rebellion,* New York, Walker & Company, 1999.

Rassmussen, A. H., *China Trader*, London, Constable and Company, 1954.

Reinders, E., *Borrowed Gods and Foreign Bodies*, Berkley, Los Angeles and London, University of California Press, 2004.

Rose, S., *For All the Tea in China*, London, Random House, 2009.

Schram, S. R., *The Political Thought of Mao Tse-Tung,* New York, Praeger, 1963.

Schurmann, F., and Schell, O. *Imperial China*, Harmondsworth, Penguin Books, 1967.

Sinn, E., (Ed.), *The Last Half Century of Chinese Overseas,* Hong Kong, Hong Kong University Press, 1998.

Spurr, R., *Excellency; The Governors of Hong Kong*, Hong Kong, Form/Asia, 1995.

Stanley, B., *The History of the Baptist Missionary Society, 1792-1992,* Edinburgh, T. & T. Clark, 1992; *The Bible and the Flag*, London, Apollos, 1990.

Taylor, J. H., *Retrospect,* Toronto, China Inland Mission, 3rd. Ed., 1902.

Teltscher, K., The High Road to China, London, Bloomsbury, 2006.

Tucker, R. A., *From Jerusalem to Irian Jaya; a biographical history of Christian Missions,* Grand Rapids, Michigan, Zondervan, 2nd Ed., 2004.

Visram, R., *Asians in Britain; 400 Years of History*, London and Sterling, VA, Pluto Press, 2002.

Wang, Y. C., *Chinese Intellectuals and the West, 1872-1949,* Cambridge, Massachusetts and London, Harvard University Press, 1960.

Welsh, F., *A History of Hong Kong*, London, Harper Collins, 1993.

Winchester, S, *The River at the Centre of the World*, London, Penguin, 1998.

Yee, C., *The Silent Traveller in Edinburgh*, London, Methuen, 1948.

Zhang, X., *The Origins of the Modern Chinese Press,* Abingdon, Routeledge, 2007.

Acknowledgements

This book has been a long time in preparation so has incurred many obligations along the way. I am grateful to my friend Tom Barron for suggesting I might explore the historical connections between Scotland and China, and the rich cast of personalities involved. The book would not have made much progress without the encouragement, and support, of Ian Aitken, Peter Freshwater, Richard Legge, Margaret and Ian Paterson and Giles Plummer, all of whom commented on various parts of the text at different times. Lucas Wun, Mandy Wong and Louisa Kwok have been my patient mentors, over many years, in introducing me to the Chinese world - I acknowledge their insights and kindness with gratitude and affection. I am particularly indebted to my friend Brian Bresnihan for his exacting comments and for sharing with me his wide experience and knowledge of Asian affairs. If the book has any merit, it arises from the input, and insights, of all of the above; any faults are mine.

I have to thank the staff of Edinburgh University Library, and the National Library of Scotland, for their outstanding courtesy and professionalism which made researching the book so hassle free. With her usual patience, Lesley Pratt helped rationalise what was, to say the least, a jumble of documents. I am indebted to her for helping create order out of chaos! I am also very grateful to Daniel Braddock, and his colleagues at CreateSpace, for their advice, and support, in the production of this book.

I would like to record huge thanks to my wife, Margaret. Without her assistance, patience and support, this book – like most other things I do - would never have been completed.

Ian Wotherspoon

Edinburgh, 2013.

CPSIA information can be obtained at www.ICGtesting.com
Printed in the USA
LVOW01s1638270913

354474LV00012B/535/P